The Unheard Voice of the Aging Parent

First published by O Books, 2010
O Books is an imprint of John Hunt Publishing Ltd., The Bothy, Deershot Lodge, Park Lane, Ropley, Hants, SO24 0BE, UK
office1@o-books.net
www.o-books.net

Distribution in:

UK and Europe
Orca Book Services Ltd
tradeorders@orcabookservices.co.uk
directorders@orcabookservices.co.uk
Tel: 01235 465521 Fax: 01235 465555
Int. code (44)

USA and Canada
NBN
custserv@nbnbooks.com
Tel: 1 800 462 6420 Fax: 1 800 338 4550

Australia and New Zealand
Brumby Books
sales@brumbybooks.com.au
Tel: 61 3 9761 5535 Fax: 61 3 9761 7095

Far East (offices in Singapore, Thailand, Hong Kong, Taiwan)
Pansing Distribution Pte Ltd
kemal@pansing.com
Tel: 65 6319 9939 Fax: 65 6462 5761

South Africa
Stephan Phillips (pty) Ltd
Email: orders@stephanphillips.com
Tel: 27 21 4489839 Telefax: 27 21 4479879

Design: Stuart Davies

ISBN: 978 1 84694 337 9

A CIP catalogue record for this book is available from the British Library.

Printed by Digital Book Print

The Unheard Voice of the Aging Parent

Carol Ball-Teplin, MPS

and

Barbara Kaplan, PhD

BOOKS

Winchester, UK
Washington, USA

CONTENTS

"Man can change and go on changing as long as he lives."
(Horney, 1942)

Dedication

We dedicate this book to three people who nurtured us, inspired us, believed in us and encouraged us to do great things. Fay Ball, Carol's mother, Cecilia Cohen, Barbara's mother, and Moshe Vardy, our guide, mentor and friend. We love you and miss you all.

Disclaimer

All references to people in the case histories we have presented are composites. If the situation seems familiar to you, rest assured they are not about you. These situations are universal and are experienced by many people at different times of their lives; even though they may seem unique to you, they are not. If you relate to anything in the book, and we hope you do, we trust that you will gain insight into your circumstances as a result.

Foreword

There are books whose topic is so extremely important that they force us to introspect and to recognize that we must change our ways. *The Unheard Voice of the Aging Parent* makes us think and consider our attitude towards the elderly. Our generation, more than many others in the past because we are living longer, has made common an event that was exceptional just three or four decades ago: people in their 50s and 60s still with elderly parents. The authors do us a big favor forcing us to focus on this current reality and to become more sensitive to the feelings and internal world of the senior adult. The 'we' I'm talking about includes all of us – educated readers and clinicians alike, especially those dealing with the elderly either in their professional offices or in the institutions where they have been interned because they cannot live alone without serious risk for themselves. For these two groups of readers, Teplin and Kaplan offer many practical suggestions on dealing with seniors for their own wellbeing and for the peace and satisfaction of those interacting with them.

The book, scholarly and easy to read, is refreshingly honest and caring. The style is unpretentious, clear, to the point and includes references to important sources. The psychodynamic flavor is quite strong and well applied in all the many clinical cases presented as confirmation of the authors' comments and written discourse. These cases are interestingly explained, without the pompous attitude of others who offer 'clinical' vignettes for illustration. The psychodynamic element appears, as I state elsewhere (Araoz, 2006), as a practical and contemporary application of psychoanalysis, in the understanding of people's behaviors, reactions, interpretations of reality, circumstances and general interactions, especially those of grown children with elderly parents. The authors convincingly refer to unconscious material in many instances without obfuscating the reader with academic vernacular. The entire twelve chapters deserve favorable comments but because of the space available, I would like to select three chapters as samples of the book. Chapter Four, on close bonds between parents and adult children, concentrates on the unique importance of these bonds during the entire lifespan of the children and tells us that older parents seeking "counseling" discover it "as a new way of approaching a problematic situation that (may have arisen) between family members." They often consider counseling beneficial "even after one session." This psychotherapy helps to reveal and evaluate frequent myths about mutual regard that manifest themselves when issues regarding what one thought or felt are examined. This point about the value of psychotherapy in adult children and older parents is further developed in Chapter Nine. It shows the flexibility that the authors have in using many methods and techniques without abandoning the basic psychodynamic principles. In ways that Wachtel (2008) would probably approve enthusiastically, they apply cognitive methods to remove patients from their NSH (negative self-hypnosis), thus avoiding the danger of clinical depression. Finally, Chapter 11 explains serious points of transference and counter-transference, emphasizing the special senior transference due to emotional loneliness and lack of the support they had in younger years. The chapter warns professionals of the delicate elements of counter-transference, agreeing with Racker (1968), the modern teacher of this subject matter, who had studied the "counter transference neurosis." The authors deserve praise for not having limited themselves to purely behavioral recommendations.

After reading this work, and having a close relative of mine in an assisted living facility, I believe it would be a good idea to ask each family member responsible for the 'patient' to use this book as a 'manual' on how to view the patient (dementia in its many forms is definitely a medical and psychological condition) and how to change one's attitude and conduct towards that individual. I stress that I consider this volume much more than a manual but because it is so uncomplicated in spite of being seriously erudite, it can also serve as a guide to all families who have a member in need of special attention and professional care.

The two authors, in a generalized psychodynamic style, help us consider things that we cannot see at first sight in dealing with elders, to reserve judgment until we have truly understood the situation and to perceive the present in terms of the patient's (and often their children's) past history and experiences which often were developmentally deficient. In this manner the book is welcome as complementing what behaviorism meritoriously but incompletely has done in innumerable opportunities. In a genuine sense the book presents a practical model of integration, as Wachtel (1997, 2008) developed and persistently proposes, that combines psychoanalysis and behavior therapy. I recognize Teplin and Kaplan for doing this so well.

In sum, as mentioned before, with the increase of people living longer, we need more mental health workers from among the many professions that are involved with this large group in our society to assist with expertise, care and dedication. This book is a worthwhile read and serves this purpose well.

Daniel L. Araoz, Ed.D., ABPP, NCC, NCPsyA
Senior Professor, Counseling and Development,
C. W. Post Campus, Long Island University.

References

Araoz, D. (2006). *The Symptom is Not the Whole Story.* New York: Other Press.

Racker, H. (1968). *Transference and Counter-transference.* New York: International Universities Press.

Wachtel, P.L. (1997). *Psychoanalysis, Behavioral Therapy and the Relational World.* Washington, D.C: American Psychological Association.

Wachtel, P.L. (2008). *Relational Theory and the Practice of Psychotherapy.* New York: Guilford Press.

Preface

The two of us worked in an agency that served individual adults and children who were diagnosed with psychological disorders and/ or substance abuse. The initial phase of our collegial relationship quickly revealed there were several commonalities. We are both female, Jewish, married with children, trained to do therapy, and each have a love of working with seniors, particularly women. Additionally, we both had experience being a caretaker of elderly mothers.

Over the next several months, at work, we continued to share breaks and dinner together and got to learn about each other's approach to treatment and interests and values. One day Carol asked Barbara if she knew a good clinical supervisor in the area. Barbara gave her the name of the man who had been supervising her. Moshe Vardy was an eighty-year-young man, with a twinkle in his eye and a demeanor and accent reminiscent of Albert Einstein. He was unique, intelligent, worldly and charming. Shortly after our discussion, he became Carol's supervisor as well. In fact, there were times when Carol and Barbara crossed paths coming and going out of Dr. Vardy's office. A few times, they even chuckled aloud as they acknowledged that there could possibly be a symbolic reason that their appointments were often scheduled back to back. Little did we know that years down the road we would be collaborating on this book!

One evening, during supervision with Carol, Moshe asked if she would be interested in co-authoring a book he was thinking of writing. Having previously read some of Carol's writing, he was impressed with her style and felt it would be complimentary to his. He mentioned that he would have asked Barbara to join this writing team; however, he knew she was inundated with completing her doctoral dissertation and he didn't want to burden her. Subsequent to that, they met and Moshe shared with her his idea for the book. Over ten years ago he had written some notes on a subject that he was very passionate about (adult sons and their fathers). Shortly after that, his wife had become ill and needed his complete attention, so he put this project aside for another time. The time was now.

Moshe described his idea for the book as the relationship conflicts between fathers and sons. Since, as a woman she could not relate to the topic, Carol felt she could not co-author the book unless she wrote from the woman's (mother and clinician) perspective. Moshe agreed. Moshe was born and raised in Hungary, and since English was not his first language, his notes were not as fluid as his thought processes. His sentence structure and grammar were written in an 'old world' style, which Carol worked to correct, edit and put into fluid, grammatically correct sentences. After working together for several months, Moshe's health began to decline, and as a result his project was again put on a shelf.

Moshe was hospitalized several times in a few short months and each time Barbara and Carol visited, they became distressed to see that he grew progressively weaker. Over the years Moshe had become more than a mentor, teacher and friend; both of us had grown very fond of him. Even though intellectually we could see that he was slipping away, in our hearts the denial had set in so firmly, we expected that he would miraculously recover and be back at his office in no time, to put up water for tea and sit and impart his clinical wisdom on two women who were eager to be in his presence. His death left a tremendous, immeasurable void for both of us.

During the mourning period, Moshe's adult children asked Carol if she would continue working on Moshe's book. Carol turned to Barbara and asked if she would consider sharing the writing with her, and they agreed to look through the notes together.

A few weeks later it was time for Carol and Barbara to have an open, honest discussion about the book and the future of writing it. They mutually felt they couldn't possibly represent the male perspective without Moshe Vardy. Instead they decided to write a book about a topic closer to their hearts, one that was very different from Moshe's original intent. The book that Carol and Barbara were to embark upon would not only represent the voices of two female clinicians, but it would also serve as a platform for the voice of the senior and adult child who had undergone therapy and addressed intergenerational problems in their families, both acquired families and families of origin.

Both Carol and Barbara had many years of clinical experience working with seniors, particularly women. They had each specialized in a variety of treatment modalities (i.e. individual, family, marital, group) and felt they had a lot of expertise to bring to the table. A few lengthy discussions about goals for the book resulted in the authors' agreement that they would incorporate some of the teachings/supervision they had acquired from Dr. Vardy, but also that their clinical stories and vignettes would not suffice. Carol and Barbara each strongly felt that they needed to include a literature search, which took them several months to complete, one that would add theoretical background to the book and document treatment approaches and the societal climate of intergenerational relationships today.

Once the table of contents, several chapters and the proposal were complete, the search for a literary agent to represent their work came next. It would be important to find someone who truly appreciated the need for the topic that addresses the unheard voice of the aging parents. With a similar energy and drive that we approached the literature search for our book, we also investigated literary agents. We spent weeks narrowing the searches down to topics in non-fiction Psychology that would highlight our project interests: sandwich generation, seniors in therapy, intergenerational conflict and aging parents and their adult children. We decided to choose Krista Goering, a woman who has her own literary agency, and someone whose first reply indicated she too had a passion for our topic. We were especially touched by her comment in an e-mail dated April 22, 2008, that "you discuss many of the issues my friends and I talk about when discussing our parents. I think this would be a great book to share with friends whose aging parents are still alive and I would be delighted to help you find a publisher."

Introduction

We consider ourselves fortunate to have been blessed with the patients who have come to us for mental health services, both for individual and group psychotherapy. Many of our patientele have been seniors, and much of the time our sessions have involved in-depth discussions and explorations of feelings about their adult children. We may have initially seen older patients as part of a married couple, a dyad of adult child and older parent, or in a women's therapy group, but often the venue changes to include or focus on individual therapy, once the history unfolds and underlying dynamics get revealed. There has certainly been an overlap in terms of issues the seniors raise, such as dependency needs, power struggles, family estrangement and conflict over parenting of grandchildren. We want to emphasize that, in almost every therapeutic case, some growth is visible during the course of therapy and family relationships vastly improve, either at the culmination of therapy or even after treatment ends. We discover that via follow-up, usually by phone and on occasion, a few patients have returned to tell their new and improved family story.

We decided that the positive changes we witnessed in our therapy sessions with our elderly patients warranted both reporting and celebrating! We also wanted to voice the opinion that, as revealed by the literature, there is an insufficient amount of material written to address how aging parents feel and think toward and about their adult sons and daughters. The elderly parents who have been a part of our practices have had interesting stories to tell and many years of wisdom to impart. We especially appreciate their openness and willingness to utilize therapy as a way to gain insight about their family relationships and also resolve conflicts, some of which have existed for many years. It is not always easy or simple to unravel the intricate feelings and past entanglements of parent and child. Yet our patients have shown courage, along with a willingness to try new patterns of behavior.

When they enter into therapy most of our elderly patients view the latter stage of their lives as the *final curtain* in a play. Will the ending be one that will be self-actualizing and fulfilling, or will it be loaded with pathos, remorse, anger and bitterness? The choice is really theirs.

Our first goal in writing this book is for our patients to define how they want their ending to be, and what they are willing to do to achieve their objective. It is our honor to be their guides on this journey.

Our second goal is for clinicians, people who do mental health counseling, to shed new light on a topic that has had little or no emphasis in the field. We also want to share our own clinical approaches that have been successful with this age group.

Why Clinical Stories?

Most of the stories presented here are closer to case histories as they represent clinical experiences from each of the authors' psychotherapy practices. They were intended to illustrate crises and resolutions, between aging parents and adult children. The adult children in our stories are between the ages of 30 and 58. Their older parents range in age between 68 and 85. Some of the stories reflect the difficulties fathers and mothers of adult children encounter while trying to fulfill their desired roles in the lives of their children. We regret that many of the stories provide negative examples, as they speak of problems, conflicts and ambivalence in the relationships, but we also acknowledge that this seems to be the nature of our clinical experiences. The brighter side is evident in that many of the parents who sought treatment learned to cope with change in their relationships with their children. Some came to terms with the loss of the illusion of what they thought the relationship was and several learned new and more fruitful ways of approaching their sons and daughters.

Some readers (i.e. adult children and aging parents) may be reading our case histories and as a result recognize their own lives. By reading about others from a distance, their identification may prove to be therapeutic or lead them into therapeutic avenues.

The stories are based on a conglomerate of real people who sought therapy as a support and a way to resolve some of the hurts and poor communication in relationships with family members. They were edited in order to disguise the identities of their characters and to protect their privacy.

Why is this topic important?

According to Shapiro (2004), the relationships between parents and children are paramount to the "psychological well-being of both generations," and is one of the most essential relationships people can have (p.127). For the purposes of our book, we find it interesting that Shapiro specifies that the parent child relationship is important to both parent and child, as the literature seems to neglect giving attention to the perspective of the parent in the relationship, particularly the aging parent. Certainly there is a lot written about the effect caretaking has on the adult child. In fact, we have newly developed terms like 'sandwich generation' and we can easily access material on 'caretaker burnout'. There exist support groups for adult children who are designated the caretaker of one or both elderly parents, but where is the mention of support groups for seniors who find themselves in a reversal of roles with their sons and daughters; feeling controlled by their children's insistence to make decisions for them? What about the experience of those older parents who have lost their sense of independence as they have to give up their homes or the notion of living alone and now have to adapt to their children's homes and family structures of their acquired families? We must not assume that it is easy for aging parents to ask for assistance from their adult children and we certainly can't assume that all of them even ask.

"The number of years of shared lives between generations is greater than at any time in history given the increase in longevity," states Van Gaalen & Dykstra (2006). According to these authors, the support given to older parents by their adult children is more driven by emotional need than any financial or normative dictate. Elderly parents need emotional support from their adult children. That's not something most of us would disagree with. The more pressing issue is whether or not there is a price to pay for that support. Another question is whether or not a bit of dignity is lost each time an older parent admits to feeling helpless, confused or lost, while navigating within a society that doesn't always acknowledge the elderly. Whether it entails a visit to the elderly parent's doctor and a need for advocacy by the adult child or simply a little help in remembering a medical fact from the parent's past, the parent may experience one or a number of different emotions about the dependency on an adult child, or even the perceived dependency. Sometimes it entails a very difficult task, like taking away an elderly parent's keys to the car and explaining why the concern. Even when the aging parent agrees with the adult child's decision (or insistence) to put an end to the parent's less than safe driving, the parent usually goes through a difficult time of loss and disappointment, which can lead to depression. Oftentimes, the parent can't express these feelings of sadness and disappointment to his or her adult son or daughter, yet it can feel easier with the aid and support of a mental health professional.

Parenting changes as we grow older. Saying to your 40-year-old child, "because I said so," or, "because I want you to," does not have the same impact as it had when your child was nine, nor is it appropriate. As parents of adult children, we need to learn how to communicate on a different level so that we do not sound like the omnipotent parents we may have seemed to be earlier in our parenting career. Otherwise we seem as obstreperous, defiant and downright silly as the Wizard in "The Wizard of Oz" when he is revealed to be a phony! As parents of adult children we need to speak to our children, if not as our peers, at least as our equals.

The one area that adult children often know little about is how their aging parents feel. Unless they talk to them about how it feels to be aging, i.e. to lose some of their functioning, some of their dignity, some of their confidence; to be afraid of becoming dependant upon them, of becoming feeble-minded, or wheel-chair bound or countless other feelings, they will continue to think of them as they were. That can translate into the adult children viewing their parents with blinders on and wrongly seeing them *now*, as strong, independent, body-able people.

The elderly patients we have seen in treatment are our heroes. They recognize that there is something that is preventing them from having a quality of life that they wish to enjoy. They don't want to wallow in pain or angst, but rather they decide to seek help. We applaud their willingness to grow and change. We are sometimes even surprised to find that our patients, who have had no earlier exposure to therapy as a way of addressing emotional problems, from their own families of origin, are open to this new venue of exploring their feelings and resolving problems within their acquired families.

Many of our patients have expressed sadness about the relationships with their child/children. They want their relationships to be closer. Many of them realize (through therapy) that they may have been less than perfect parents and desire to 'right the wrongs' they have made with their offspring. We have found that utilizing Cognitive Behavioral Therapy (CBT) assists us in guiding them towards the path of reconciling with their loved ones. We have helped them through changing the way they express themselves, letting go of the negativity and critical, fault-finding tactics that haven't worked for them in the past, and certainly don't work today. Many of our patients have found it very difficult to change the patterns established over a lifetime. However, with encouragement, education and enlightenment, they embrace the prospect of a renewed, loving relationship with their children in their 'not-so-golden' years. They are taught how to give up the behaviors that were destructive or just not productive for themselves or others in the family, anymore.

Many adult children live in a vacuum concerning their parents. As long as both parents are 'intact', meaning they live together and take care of each other and there are no overt demands on their adult children for care, financial assistance, or even companionship, everything goes smoothly. The adult children, as long as their parents are reasonably healthy, live in a sense of denial as to their parents' eminent failing health and eventual demise. As an example, our associate's forty-year-old daughter keeps making her mother promise that she will never die. Now of course, they both know that this is impossible, but just by her daughter making her promise not to die, tells her that she will miss her tremendously, appreciates her and that she loves her. This is reassuring to our colleague and comforting for her to know how close her daughter feels.

In the book "Adult Children and Their Parents: The Ties That Keep on Binding", by Matti K. Gershenfeld, the author said: "How you treat your parents is a model for how you will be treated when your children become adults. We often think our parents did it wrong and we will do it right. We think that, with our greater education and worldly experience, as well as our recognition of how important parenting is, we will act to our children in such a way that when they grow up, we will have warm, close, ongoing relationships. Their observation of our actions has greater salience than anything we can say as parents. What is especially important is that adult children have an ongoing, caring relationship with their parents so that, in the next generation, their children will possibly have a model of how to act towards them." We, as clinicians, fervently believe that an intergenerational focus in therapy, with the older parent and the middle-aged child, is not only useful but essential to the process of strengthening family relationships. We have noticed, in countless sessions that family dynamics get re-enacted over and over within generations, or at best, surface with common threads that may go unnoticed until there is a crisis or a conflict that seems too large to tackle.

Therefore, to clarify our dual purpose in writing this book, we wrote it for adult children to more readily hear and understand the feelings their elderly parents experience at this late stage of their lives, and for elderly parents to find hope that they *can* change and improve relationships with their children. Our examples will show that it is never too late to have a happier life. We also wrote this book for clinicians who have been reluctant to treat the elderly due to preconceived notions that working with this population is depressing or of little therapeutic value. Our experiences to the contrary are astounding! We offer this book as proof positive that the elderly population possesses a unique and powerful source of wisdom, strength and eagerness to embrace the therapeutic process as a means of improving their quality of life, and are a joy to work with!

1. Supervision with Moshe Vardy

"Please, describe the patient to me and help me know the person. I want to hear about the way she or he looks and interacts with you as though you are painting a picture, and I want to know how you feel with this person in the room. I also want to know what kinds of concerns you have for future therapeutic work with the individual and some diagnostic impressions. What do you think the therapeutic relationship will be like?"

The above is a typical scenario depicting how clinical supervision following the initial session with a new patient would begin with Dr. Michael Vardy, whom we knew as 'Moshe'. The descriptions helped him get a distinct view of the patient, through our eyes, and it somehow brought the therapy patient into the room symbolically so he or she could be an integral part of his or her own treatment. Sometimes the descriptions were so specific that our supervisor told us he had a very good conception of the person we were treating, almost as though he had seen a snapshot. Each of us had the good fortune to work with Moshe for a period of 1–2 years, and the blessing of becoming a colleague and good friend following that supervision also proved to be very meaningful.

Dr. Vardy's orientation was existential in nature. He strongly believed that one of the most essential things to uncover is the meaning to the patient, whether talking about life or death. He also believed that we must not shy away from painful feelings as we can learn and grow further in our humanness if we embrace it, and help our patients do the same. To some, it may have seemed that Moshe did not always sympathize with painful emotions, but we knew differently. He didn't want that pain to overcome the individual, as there is much to understand about life through suffering, and it was his strength that helped us truly see that. Spillers (2007) states it this way: "how we embrace these challenges and find meaning in our lives becomes part of our spiritual journeys," (p. 191). Another very important element in his existential clinical supervision was the understanding of the relationship between the therapist and the patient and the hope that the supervision would assist the therapist in developing a deeper awareness of self, in addition to the patient, via the analysis of the supervisee's defenses as well as those of the patients. In discussing the more difficult issues a supervisee brings to the table (i.e. what he or she constitutes as a failure in treatment, shortcoming in oneself, or admission that one does not know something clinical), a therapist inevitably experiences growth in their abilities and more successes with their patients.

Supervision with Moshe was never dull or repetitive and that was true even if we used a similar structure at first to identify the patient and his or her pathology and psychodynamics. Our supervisor knew that it was sometimes challenging to bring a clinical supervision issue in, yet those were the ones we learned the most from, if we did take that step, overcoming fears and anxieties in the process. Sometimes our supervisor asked us to talk about something that entailed taking a risk in that it might expose a personal belief, value or feeling that may not be in sync with his. The material raised by either one of us was always received with a nonjudgmental reaction and it in turn encouraged us to bring more issues to our supervision that may have previously gone unsaid.

Yet, he always knew when the lines of supervision were at risk for getting blurred, lines that should direct a clinician to personal therapy and, believe us, he directed us there if the need arose. In addition, he made suggestions as to what we might want to address in our own therapy and he made sure to follow up with us to inquire about whether the issue was resolved. The issues that we found difficult to raise involved counter-transference and required addressing our own personal journey towards the maintenance of good mental health. We acknowledged that a good check and balance of any possible projections and possible avoidance of topics or issues is essential.

There was little inhibition about bringing in almost anything once trust developed in the supervisory relationship with Moshe. In fact, he never raised an eyebrow no matter how personal the topic about the patient was, how deeply it needed to be explored and or how it may have differed with the style and approach he had learned several decades earlier. Sometimes we brought in our fantasies or dreams about patients, while other times we initiated an exploration of our hypotheses, theories or clinical treatment goals. Either way, we left his office feeling there was an overabundant amount of material covered and a wealth of wisdom imparted. It was additionally no surprise to leave the office with a book, whether old or current, that he assigned for reading and for discussion in upcoming supervision sessions.

We also left his office feeling a lightness of heart much of the time, as our supervisor knew how and when to inject humor, a humor that reminded us of the importance of feeling joy about life in general and knowing we are not alone with any feelings we may have, as treating professionals delivering what is sometimes a difficult service to others. There was also the humor that accompanies the absurdities in life, even the ones about us, our opinions or the choices we make. In sessions with our supervisor, we were able to laugh at ourselves in a way that did not hamper us or play havoc with our self-esteem.

Moshe was devoted to the work of Irvin Yalom, the psychiatrist who was existential in his thinking. One of the last books our supervisor read was Yalom's "Love's Executioner". In it Yalom discusses the meaning of "existence pain" to be the kind of pain that is always there, making all human beings anxious about the inevitability of death. Even just mentioning this reminds us that Moshe had little difficulty talking about death and he brought an unusual level of comfort in discussing it into his supervision. There were also times in which he was able to conceptualize that a patient's behavior linked back to a fear of death or losing a loved one, and this proved to be enlightening, especially when working with the older patient.

Moshe taught us not to avoid talking about death and loss, with him, our patients and also with loved ones. He felt that people could certainly learn from maintaining this kind of openness and those patients in the last years of their lives often do not have anyone to talk to about this inevitable part of life.

Moshe told us that he also idealized Yalom for his ability to admit his own vulnerability and failings with patients and Moshe exemplified this very behavior with his supervisees and his patients. In fact, there were times in which our supervisor repeated a story many times because it reflected what he considered to be an error with a patient. It always seemed that what was most important to him was that he, as the clinician, learned from the failure or what he termed "the miss" with the patient.

It was not unusual for Moshe to assign reading in supervision and it was refreshing to hear a professional with more than 45 years experience say that he continued to read and learn about his field. As academia remained essential to Moshe all of his life, he made sure to bring an educational component in to supervision. He told us that it is paramount that we know theoretical background as a foundation to diagnosing and conceptualizing our patients, their personal thoughts and their world views. Completing educational programs and acquiring degrees should not, in his estimation, preclude one from continuing to read psychological material or even find supporting evidence for diagnostic impressions. It also wasn't enough to refer back to the DSM IV (Diagnostic Statistical Manual used by clinicians) for a list of symptom clusters for any particular diagnosis. Instead, we were directed to clinical textbooks that provided theoretical explanations of pathology and interventions that might be appropriate. Our supervisor also imparted his clinical wisdom at every turn and shared clinical stories that were triggered back into memory by the many different cases we brought to supervision. His retention for what he learned during his many years of practice, teaching and supervision seemed limitless and explains part of the primary reason that supervision provided such a rich environment for maturation of a therapist.

Our supervisor also taught us about "turning points". He used this term to mean those moments in the therapeutic relationship in which there is an actual turn for the better. It may be that the patient allows the intimacy to develop with the therapist and he or she reveals a secret or painful feeling that had been tucked away, or it may mean that the patient comes to truly believe that the therapist cares more about him or her than originally thought. Moshe wanted to write an article about "turning points" but his own health had started to get compromised before he had the time to put it in writing. It is, in part, for this reason that we decided to write this book in his honor and a discussion about supervision seemed poignant.

Moshe wanted to write a book about senior fathers and their adult sons. It was his vision to present to the reader, whether the practitioner or the layman, a view from his perspective of the intergenerational problems the male family members encounter and the ways in which he saw fit to treat these issues. We, as seasoned clinicians, felt compelled to represent our own therapeutic communities which are comprised of both genders and more heavily populated with female patients. We additionally felt it was necessary to embody the voice of our patients, male and female, within the context of our gender, rather than try and present the original topic our supervisor had wanted to pursue: the relationships of fathers and sons. We both always felt that our supervisor clearly saw the importance of acknowledging the wealth of knowledge to be gleaned from therapeutic conversations with seniors.

Moshe did not view age as a deterrent to being active or

involved in life and learning. Instead, he inspired us, via his own role modeling and his sharing of clinical experience taken from working with the older population, to view old age as a time for creativity and forming close bonds with others, especially family members. We couldn't agree more and therefore approach our senior patients with enthusiasm for gaining knowledge about their family relationships and their perceptions about the aging process. We also continue to learn from them and seek each other out for peer supervision, so that kind of learning is also never lost.

2. Father Hunger

The term 'father hunger' is one that was first coined by Herzog (2001). Dr. Herzog referred to this term as "an affective state of considerable tenacity and force", one that leaves a child in a state of continual longing for normal involvement from a father figure (p.35). We use the term to describe when a patient exhibits a yearning for the paternal love object that was rarely or never experienced. This may be the result of a single parent household or caused by the father's long work hours, frequent business trips or any other such scenarios. It also may be that the father was physically at home but was emotionally absent. In any case, father hunger can create a huge deficit in the adult child feeling lovable or whole.

Is it Husband Envy?

Married at twenty to a man eleven years her senior, Regina had four children before her 30th year. Her husband, an austere, undemonstrative, emotionally distant man, was the second of seven children raised by a stern, harsh, German immigrant father, who had no time for his children. Not surprisingly, he modeled his fatherhood after his parents. He wanted dinner on the table and the kids ready for bed when he returned from work each night, and his weekends were spent working on his stamp collection and playing golf.

Regina explained that she did everything in her power to educate, support, love and nurture her children, with the bare minimum of involvement from her husband. He was the unsmiling, critical and punishing parent; she was the forgiving, demonstrative and benevolent mom.

All during the children's growing up years they continually sought their father, and were disappointed to realize that their father was emotionally and physically absent from most of the events in their lives. He lived by the edict that 'children should not be seen or heard!' Regina sometimes made excuses for him, but eventually allowed her anger and resentment at feeling like a "single married mother" to filter through.

After their children married and the grandchildren started arriving, Regina came into therapy with an unusual presenting problem. She explained it this way: she couldn't understand how her adult children would bend over backwards to gain their father's approval and love. He had a less than minimal role in their upbringing and yet, there they were, all adults and they practically ignore her and fawn over him. She didn't understand the dynamic involved here, and she felt jealous of their attention and devotion to him. She repeated, "It just doesn't seem right."

After several weeks of therapy, Regina was eventually able to understand the concept that her children understood her love was unconditional and that their father's was an unknown. It stood to reason that they felt they did not have to work at getting her love so they didn't try. Their father was another story. He was a challenge, a mystery, an enigma that they thought they could solve if they were persistent and relentless in conveying their adoration to him. What they could not comprehend was that no matter what they did or didn't do, their father was incapable of giving them what they hungered for, his love, and it wasn't their fault, or his.

At one point in our therapy Regina had an 'aha' moment. She reported that when she was dating her husband she knew that he was undemonstrative and didn't or couldn't show his emotions. She knew that he was obsessed with his stamp collections and playing golf. She knew these things but hoped if she loved him enough he would change and shower on her the attention and affection that she so sorely missed in the marriage. We spoke about her feelings of failure, low self-esteem and rejection when she realized her love did not effect a change in him. It was then that she realized that the same dynamic, which was present in her early life with her husband, was present now in her children. They hoped that if they "loved him enough, he would return that love!"

The responsibility to change is inherent in each of us. If her husband was comfortable with his life the way it was, no matter how much love she or their children showered on him, he would remain the same, and it wasn't her fault. We continued therapy for some time, working on issues as they came up and helping to create a healthy self-image for Regina.

Bridging the Gay Gap

Sidney was hesitant about telling me, at first, that his son Larry was gay. It seemed like he wanted me to guess, based on his many hints, such as: Larry introduced me to his "partner", and "Larry wasn't like other guys". It wasn't until the second month of treatment that Sidney revealed to me that his son was homosexual and that it was something he couldn't initially accept. According to Sidney, who was 77 at the time he came to therapy, he had envisioned a certain lifestyle for his only son and he included himself in that vision. He saw himself looking proudly at his son's traditional life, married to a woman who would bear his future grandchildren. All of that didn't materialize and instead Larry was living with his lover, Ron. Every time Sidney went to see his son and his partner, an argument ensued between father and son.

The strife between them built and built until Larry asked Sidney to come to one of his therapy sessions. Sidney obliged because he wanted to resolve the conflict between them, some of which he didn't comprehend. According to my patient, the session went well, however, the therapist suggested individual therapy for Sidney and he wasn't amenable at that time. It wasn't an easy task for Sidney to discuss, in therapy with me, what happened in detail in that family session, but he tried his best to recount the exchange.

That session with Larry's therapist revealed that once Larry told his parents he was gay, his mother ceased being warm to him. Sidney's relationship with his wife was very passive. Whatever she wanted, he more or less agreed with rather than 'rocking the boat'. When his wife decided not to have much to do with her son after the disclosure, Sidney, being submissive, went along with her decision to punish Larry by keeping distant from him, even though he disagreed with his wife. His wife never discussed her feelings openly and died before ever taking the opportunity to tell Larry how she felt. Larry was more upset at Sidney, however, feeling that his dad had taken his mother's side when in fact he had come to accept his son's gay lifestyle and partner choice, but did not feel comfortable going against his wife's wishes. Sidney had a great deal of regret about the collusion with his wife but it seemed to be that Larry was not about to forgive him after all the years that elapsed.

Sidney did not seek therapy with me because of feelings about Larry's sexual orientation. He came to see me because he was grieving over the loss of his wife Shirley, who had died of a massive heart attack at the age of 72. At the suggestion of his family physician, Sidney first went to a bereavement group for individuals who lost spouses and after eight weeks of group, he and his counselor agreed that he needed something more. Sidney felt lost and alone and was finding it particularly hard to reach out to Larry for support. The loss of his wife brought with it the memory of the close relationship he once had with his son. Now for the first time Sidney wanted to thoroughly explore his feelings and learn how to cope with what little relationship he could salvage with Larry.

According to my patient, everything he did as a father was wrong or misconstrued by Larry. Sidney explained that when he sent a holiday card to his son and Ron, Larry got upset that Ron's name didn't appear first on the card, as it meant to him that his father didn't approve of his partner. Another time Sidney left a message on Ron's cell, wishing them both a Happy New Year, something he thought would please his son. Instead of receiving it warmly, Larry became angry at Sidney and later told him that his actions were meant to impress Ron and that the intent was not sincere. There were numerous instances like those mentioned above and eventually the communication between Sidney and Larry became almost nonexistent. Sidney expressed feeling that the loss of contact was most painful now that his wife was gone. He didn't know how to bridge the gap between him and his adult son, and he wanted so much to be close to him, especially in his latter years.

In our sessions Sidney kept saying that he wanted to connect with his son Larry. Although he seemed sincere, when questioned, Sidney revealed that he hadn't contacted Larry in the last year because he felt sure that his overtures would be rejected, and he was afraid of another confrontation. We discussed several different ways that he could safely contact his son without the dreaded confrontation and finally decided that e-mail might work. I sent Sidney home to compose his thoughts, and then write them.

The following week Sidney showed up at my office refreshed and relaxed. I commented on his mood and he replied, "It felt good to get my feelings about my son on paper and out of my gut." Together we read what Sidney had written; modified them to include the feelings he had expressed which we had explored in treatment and came up with the following letter:

> Dear Larry, I am writing to tell you that I miss you. Clearly, we have had misunderstandings in the past, and if I hurt you I want you to know that I am sorry. It was never my intention to hurt you. I would like the opportunity to go ahead. I know I can't erase the past but I sincerely want to be a better father to you, one that you can rely on. I look forward to hearing from you soon. Dad.

In a report by Silverstein, Parrott & Bengston (1995) they cite: "A persistent theme in many respondents' reports is a desire for their relationships with the other generation to be more satisfying. This is important. It is also important to note that although families may acknowledge tension, disagreements and conflicts, at the same time they can also report high levels of intergenerational solidarity, indicating there is affection, contact and mutual support."

When Larry received the letter from his father, he was reluctant to open it. Although he was comfortable in the lifestyle he had chosen with his partner Ron, there were times that he experienced pangs of remorse about his lack of closeness with his father. Now that his mother was gone, he often wondered how his father was doing, but squelched that little spark inside him that wanted to reach for the phone. "I'm better off this way – without having to sense my father's disapproval and rejection. It's easier not to have to continuously squabble with him and attempt to root out his hidden agenda each time."

There were times after he spent the evening with Ron's family and they returned to their apartment Larry experienced a deep sadness. He missed having a caring parent. He envied Ron's relationship with his loving family, who accepted him as he was from the minute he came out of the closet. Ron's parents told him straight out that they were disappointed that there would never be a daughter-in-law or grandchildren from their only child. They released their expectations of the extended family and acknowledged that their son's ultimate happiness was their primary concern. His own life seemed so empty by contrast. He longed for a closeness with his father that his partner Ron had with his parents.

He snapped out of his reverie and slowly opened the letter. He was touched by the earnestness and honesty of his father's words and felt warmed by the simplicity of his request to go forward and become a better father to Larry. The proverbial ball was now in his court. This could be an opportunity to finally enter into a loving relationship with his father once again or a chance to smash his father to pieces by refusing his apology and telling him to go to hell. The choice was not difficult. He reached for the phone, dialed his father's number and said, "I miss you too, Dad."

In summary, as clinicians we are in agreement that this kind of reparative work may not be easy, but the possible gain for the adult child/older parent relationship is immeasurable.

Abuse Memories That Emerge

Then there was Sharon, who was a young woman in her early thirties at the time she first entered treatment. She brought with her an obvious sadness, which she attributed to her feeling of losing the 'favorite' position in the eyes of her father. The patient said that she went from being "daddy's little princess" to being "dethroned", as though she had lost not only her royal position, but her father's love as well. Sharon didn't know if her position had likely been usurped by her younger brother Jonathan, who was born when the patient was 5 years old, or if her father had been too distracted by other things. The patient had decided that, whatever the reason, she was going to forgive her father "and move on". She wanted to bridge the gap and become closer to her brother and possibly see him more regularly. Most importantly, she didn't want to continue carrying around resentment toward her father as it affected their interactions. "It's like there is cool air between us, whenever we get together," Sharon said.

I clearly felt that, after two years of therapy, Sharon had placed her feelings of sibling rivalry toward Jonathan and resentment toward her father into a realistic, healthier perspective. For example, she came to feel that her father may not have realized that she felt ignored or that his attention was unevenly weighted toward her brother when he was a baby. I helped Sharon, with a cognitive-behavioral approach, to examine thoughts she had that may have been irrational about losing her father's love and being replaced by her brother. I thought she had, in her words, "moved on". She sought me out years later and explained that she was now in her early forties and seemed to be "in crisis". She described the presenting problem this way.

Sharon was consumed with feelings of hatred toward her father and fear about the prospect of marrying her boyfriend, a man named Richard, whom she dated for several years. Memories had surfaced about her father sexually touching her, when she was 4 or 5 years old. These memories were causing Sharon to obsess about ways to retaliate against her father and she was further troubled when she noticed a growing feeling, an aversion toward her fiancé Richard. Sharon stated that she couldn't make love to Richard, feeling the way she did toward him, her father and men in general. She wondered how much longer Richard would tolerate her rejections. Sharon also said that she would occasionally force herself to have sex with her boyfriend despite her feelings and, as a result, she would become depressed and agitated.

I was able to assist Sharon in telling her boyfriend about the sexual abuse she remembered experiencing with her dad, and helped her to find the right words to communicate to Richard what she needed from him emotionally, since that would help her with sharing physical intimacy with him.

The therapy was also useful in helping Sharon work through her ambivalent feelings toward her father of anger about the memories, and yet longing for his closeness and love. She needed to decide whether or not she felt the need to confront him. Sharon's father was, at the time, in his early seventies and her mother was deceased. Sharon wanted some kind of relationship with her father, and she told me that there still existed the chance that her memories did not completely and accurately depict the past. The prospect of losing the father and daughter relationship totally was the most frightening possibility to Sharon.

In our work together Sharon had to establish what she would stand to gain by confronting her father and what she stood to lose if she did not. After several weeks of intensive work in therapy her decision was clear. To move on with her life, she needed to work out her feelings with her father in a safe, supportive environment. At that point, she invited her father to join her in a therapy session. Sharon was surprised to learn that her father also felt the readiness to work on improving their relationship. He was willing to share with both me and Sharon the shame he experienced every time he looked at his daughter and the fear of losing her that consumed him. He did not deny the abuse yet he also admitted that he had been in denial for many years. Sharon found out for the first time that her father had been in extensive therapy and it had greatly benefited him. In fact, Sharon expressed that she felt she was "reaping the rewards" of her father's therapeutic work. The session we had was only the tip of the iceberg as it certainly opened a long overdue dialogue between parent and child. We continued joint therapy and worked on mending and healing the damage that had been done over the years by the shame and the silence between them. Sharon shared that she continued to have weekly dinners with her father, and from what we gleaned from this both she and her father were doing their own reparative work and it was paying off indeed.

Our clinical experience has taught us that many fathers today want a good deal of involvement with their adult children. Likewise, we also see many fathers who have troubled relationships with their children and these conflicts, in many instances, are chronic in nature and have not been given attention in the past. One of the most common problems is strained communication between the generations. Sometimes the aging father has given up or feels helpless in terms of what he can do to effect a positive change with his son or daughter.

Another common problem is the lack of attention from a

father that can be blamed in part on the busy lifestyle he had when raising his children. Working long hours, often six days a week, sometimes traveling for weeks at a time, separated them from their family. They were continually trying to balance the rising cost of living by working to keep one step ahead of the bills. By the time the chaos has quieted down, the children had married and had children of their own, with little time to spend with their dad.

Often the elderly parent, now in the 'look back on my life' stage, takes stock of the things in their life that went well and those things that they regret, and may feel guilt or remorse for the relationships within the family that they failed to nurture and develop. The words to the song, "Cat's in the Cradle", comes back to haunt the men of the 50's, 60's, 70's and 80's who tried to build a career, very often at the expense of bonding with their children. Now they are retired and have the time to review their lives, they mourn the loss of a meaningful connection with their children that they sacrificed for the sake of their careers. They sadly say, "I did it for them," but the reality is that their children suffered in the process, and now they are all suffering the loss.

One of the most common problems as a result of the father's workaholic past is strained communication with their children. Sometimes the aging father has given up or feels helpless in terms of what he can do to effect a positive change with his son or daughter. We have seen elderly men work through their feelings of guilt and shame in a therapeutic setting, until they feel ready to express their thoughts in a safe environment with their children. This takes a tremendous amount of courage, and we applaud the patients we have worked with who were able to bridge the gap, ask for forgiveness when they felt it was necessary, and forge a budding relationship with their estranged children. We are not saying it was an easy road, but we do know that the rewards were remarkable for all concerned. In our practice we have learned that it is never too late to endeavor to establish a meaningful connection with one's children, if the parent is able to convey their sincere desire to do so without a hidden agenda.

3. Not Black or White: Grey

It may take a few trips to one's local library before the book "Walking on Eggshells" is available as it is quite popular today. It's no surprise since the book describes the relationship problems between adult children and their parents. This topic seems to be a much needed topic for many people to read and learn about, possibly, in some cases, as a way of improving the relationships, and probably, in many instances, as a way of validating what was being felt by both parents and adult children. Jane Isay, the author of the book, interviewed approximately seventy-five adult children and their parents. Some of the parent-child dyads were far younger than our targeted population, but the perspective of the adult child and aging parent certainly had a substantial voice in this enlightening and therapeutic book and its qualitative research.

The author talks about the hardships faced by adult children and their parents and the importance for parents to understand the discomfort felt by adult children returning to live at home, after living apart for many years. In our practices, we have seen several situations in which adult children return to their parents' home after a failed marriage, financial problems or loss of employment. Parents often have a tendency to resume old familiar patterns of expecting their sons and daughters to be continually accountable for their whereabouts or divulging intimate details about their lives like they did when they were young. Adult children, particularly older adults, may feel their freedom being compromised as they are no longer used to such accountability and sharing of feelings. Isay believes, and we strongly agree, that the adult child and aging parent can meet halfway at these times, while making an effort to appreciate and respect the unique needs of one another, needs that change as we continue to mature and live independently. There are new levels of closeness and relating that need to be navigated in this family dyad and oftentimes it can feel like a re-enactment of the adolescent child and parent relationship. The parent and adult child have to find a balance of power and involvement that makes sense for both. They need to clearly see this developmental stage (of adult child and aging parent) as uniquely different from the adolescent child and parent unit they once were. The middle-aged son or daughter is not being rebellious and the senior parent does not intend to have the same amount of control he or she once had.

In the book, *Walking on Eggshells,* the author speaks about parents' frustration when they are at odds with their adult children in the latter stages of their lives. She goes on to say it isn't easy for parents to construe their grown children's behavior when they are not returning their phone calls, when they criticize them, fight with them, and show a certain disdain. But most often the love is there – hiding in plain sight. "We just need to remember that their expressions of resentment or anger don't equal lack of love." (Pg 34)

Marilyn Unmarried

The following vignette exemplifies one woman's struggle in her relationship with her adult son moving back home. Marilyn, a stately woman of 68, came into treatment when she was "at her wit's end" with a family problem. A single mother of five, her husband left when her youngest son was diagnosed as developmentally disabled. "He couldn't accept the fact that his son was less than perfect," says Marilyn, "so he abandoned all of us." Left with no financial support from her husband, little emotional or financial support from her parents, Marilyn was devastated. With no skills, no education and very little self-esteem, she searched for ways to support her large family. "I applied for an entry-level corporate job and stayed for twenty-five years, creeping up the ladder to a very prestigious position by the time I retired."

During those twenty-five years Marilyn's family grew to adulthood. Four of her children married, some with children, and her youngest son was placed in a group home nearby. "My home could never be described as an empty nest, since the children visited frequently and there was always something bubbling on the stove, or baking in the oven when they arrived. I feel very close to my children, and adore my seven grandchildren," said Marilyn. She was proud of her children's accomplishments as well. "One is a marketing executive with a major advertising firm, one a director of an assisted living facility, one is a "stay at home mom, and one a dentist," sighed Marilyn.

The bomb fell when her dentist son was arrested on insurance fraud charges. Life as the family knew it was over, Marilyn's bubble was not only burst, it was shattered. "Maybe I was in denial, but I didn't believe that the changes in his personality and the erratic behavior he had displayed were signs of criminal activity. Whenever I asked him about his moods and the extreme changes in his demeanor he explained it away as simply stress on the job and in the marriage, nothing more." Subsequent to his arrest, his license was revoked, his wife left him and he lost his house. Clinically depressed, stripped of everything of value, with nowhere else to go, Jonathan moved back home with Marilyn at age 38.

From our perspective, Marilyn was not emotionally prepared for what was to follow. Her son Jonathan continued on a destructive path. He fell into a depression and rarely left the house. He slept and watched TV all day and sleeplessly paced the house all night. Although we are not fond of the term, Marilyn seemed to remain an "enabler" for quite a while. Therapy helped her see that she needed to acknowledge her past actions and then examine her motives.

From Marilyn's descriptions of the acrid odor in his bedroom, the long hours he slept in the morning and his lack of motivation, we surmised that Jonathan was smoking marijuana. We needed to educate Marilyn about what it means for someone to medicate themselves with a substance as she had no prior exposure to this. Jonathan was always asking his mother for money for schemes or work projects that did not materialize. Marilyn fought her inkling to see the truth about her son's problems, and of course the more she was privy to them, the worse it was for her. She said, "I wouldn't know this much about drugs if I didn't live with my son and I wish I didn't know half of it." On one occasion, Jonathan asked Marilyn to front him money to buy a cell phone and service plan, just until he could work and pay for it independently. Marilyn convinced herself that her son needed the phone for business reasons and that he would come through and would pay her back when he "got on his feet". When Marilyn saw the first bill for $500 and then the next for $680, she knew that this arrangement was destined to fail. She realized that she had become further and further in debt because of Jonathan's schemes and this pattern could not continue.

Only to make matters worse, she looked in her liquor cabinet and discovered all the bottles of liquor were drunk and water was substituted to make them look untouched. It was then that she realized that Jonathan was abusing alcohol as well as drugs. As if Marilyn wasn't stressed enough, this proof that her son was using alcohol made her even more upset with the situation. It was at this lowest point in her mental health that her other adult children confronted her about her "need for tough love" with Jonathan and insisted that she set reasonable limits. They wanted her to be consistent in her dealings with him so that he would know, first of all, that she was adhering to her principles and would not allow him to continue to live the lifestyle he had become accustomed to. They all agreed that he needed to get help or get out, and she needed to be firm with this.

Her children told her over dinner one night that she needed to say "no" to Jonathan no matter how painful it would be for her. They revealed to her that they had been setting limits with

Jonathan for several years, as asking them for money to get him out of a jam was not uncommon. In fact, it even placed her oldest daughter in debt for a short period of time, since, despite his promises that he would repay his debt to her, the loan was never repaid.

We knew that a cognitive behavioral approach might be helpful to Marilyn and so we offered her assertiveness training. Marilyn accepted the offer to learn this communication tool, in combination with an agreement to attend weekly meetings at Al-anon. We believed strongly that Marilyn needed the 12-step program, and the support of a group of people who had 'walked in her shoes', to further assist her in not being an enabler to her son. She needed to gain strength in facing a very difficult task that was to come: confronting the problem head on, while taking care of herself in the process.

With the help of this therapeutic treatment plan, Marilyn was ready for a crisis intervention specialist. We referred her to a colleague who was specially trained in providing crisis intervention in the home. He met with Marilyn, Jonathan, her adult children, and Jonathan's closest male friend. Prior to the meeting at Marilyn's house a bed was secured at a rehabilitation facility.

We believe that the continuing support of her Al-anon friends provides motivation for her to work hard in the therapeutic setting. The therapeutic work, which was insight-oriented, helped her begin to understand that enabling her son, turning her back on his inappropriate behavior with drugs and alcohol, did not make her a 'good mother', just as arranging for the intervention did not make her a 'bad mother'.

As seasoned clinicians, we must know when we need either a higher level of care for our patients or their family members and when the expertise of other professionals is required in order to give the patient the best opportunity at achieving stabilization and good mental health. What remained to address, after this intervention, was the personal aftermath for Marilyn. Despite our therapeutic recommendation, Marilyn refused to go any further at this time. Sometimes this happens and a patient dictates an earlier termination that we feel is warranted. We learn to accept that the patient's readiness may not always fit our anticipated timeline.

Living Together

One of the greatest barriers to launching a respectful, close relationship with adult children is the lack of establishing healthy boundaries when they are young. However, it is our experience that it is never too late to put those boundaries in place.

Susan, a sixty-something divorced mother of two came into treatment because of the strain and tension she was living with. She explained that after her divorce it became difficult to pay the mortgage and household bills on her salary alone. Her daughter, Lucy, married and the mother of two children, suggested that she and her family move in with Susan to ease the financial burden. After some deliberation Susan agreed and the two arranged to share all expenses evenly.

In an article by Martin Turcotte in *Canadian Social Trends* entitled: "Parents with Adult Children Living at Home" (2006), he states that parents playing host to their adult children has become a more common living arrangement in recent years. In many of these scenarios, the picture drawn is one of frustrated parents enduring a situation they had neither planned nor prepared for. Stress, discouragement and eventual conflicts are said to be part of the routine in these households.

Susan reported that in her experience a mother should not be witness to her child's marriage and parenthood on a daily basis. It's not fair to either one. She got to see how cranky her daughter's husband was, what a poor housekeeper her daughter was and how spoiled their children were. Her house became a battlefield; doors slamming, people screaming at each other and everyone's privacy intruded upon. They would sit down and try to iron out their problems, and things would be better for a few days, maybe a week, but then like a rubber band they would snap back to the original configuration – chaos! Susan found the situation to be intolerable.

By the time Susan began therapy she was barely talking to her daughter and felt like a stranger in her own house. Her job, as an office manager of a huge orthopedic office, seemed like her only refuge. Originally, one of her primary motives to agree to the shared household with her daughter was to ease her loneliness after the divorce. When we began treatment Susan revealed that her daughter's family did not even eat their meals with her. She cooked her food and ate alone to avoid conflict and aggravation from "them".

At first, the separation from the family (i.e. eating meals alone and watching separate TV's in the evening) worked for Susan, but after time, she started to feel isolated and alone, while her resentment brewed more and more. Part of our work together centered on helping Susan to recognize what she was in fact feeling. Before long we realized the depth of complexities to her emotions. Remaining removed from the family lowered her anxiety in some respects, yet she also harbored angry, sad feelings about the fact that her daughter perpetuated the isolation by ignoring the situation; *ignoring her*.

Another aspect to treatment was to assist the patient in exploring in what ways she wanted to be a part of the family. She needed to decide whether the living arrangements were to be temporary or permanent, and also to be able to say what she needed and what she was willing to give to make the arrangement work. Susan's personal growth was at stake. Asserting herself to say what she was feeling was something she was not inclined to do all throughout her adult years. She recalled that such behavior only created more depression and maintained her self-esteem at a low level. Susan realized that for many years she had developed a pattern of using work as a defense against forming healthy personal relationships at home. She revealed that she usually opted to work longer hours to escape from the miserable relationship she had with her husband. The current change in her living situation brought back memories of the way she raised her daughter. She realized that she wasn't there for her daughter during a critical time in Lucy's life. By using work to distance herself from her abusive husband, she distanced herself from her daughter as well. For the first time, feelings of guilt surfaced and Susan felt overwhelmed and in need of support.

In our treatment Susan recalled being raised by very strict, old-world parents. She believed that the parenting she received from them was faulty, and thought, "When I have children I will correct the deficit." As a result, she raised her children in the exact opposite manner and style of her parents, and was overly permissive towards them. At this stage in her life she wanted to garner cooperation and respect from her daughter and knew that she had some serious work to do on herself in order to achieve that goal.

To begin with, Susan needed to list the things that were important to her right now. This was very difficult for her since she said she had no clear definition of what her wants and needs were. One thing she did know was that she valued her privacy and could not tolerate anyone invading that privacy. That was a great place for us to start. We decided that she would keep her bedroom door closed and Susan would tell her family not to enter her room without her permission, and that she would do the same for them. As simple as this sounded, Susan had a hard time finding her 'voice' when it came to actually advocating for herself. A few days later, Susan returned looking victorious! She described how wonderful she felt when her daughter thought that this was a good idea. This little compromise gave Susan the courage to continue forging ahead toward setting more goals and establishing greater boundaries.

In a report by Silverstein, Parrott & Bengston (1995) they cite: "A persistent theme in many respondents' reports is a desire for their relationships with the other generation to be more satisfying. This is important. It is also important to note that although families may acknowledge tension, disagreements and conflicts, at the same time they can also report high levels of intergenerational solidarity, indicating there is affection, contact and mutual support."

As aging parents, there is a tendency to continue with the same type of parenting style as we had used when they were younger. Experience shows us that this doesn't work. The shift we have to make when our children are adolescents pales by comparison to the shift that needs to be put into play when they are middle-aged. Our children now have their own children and they feel as if they have mastered the 'parenting' game. Any suggestion that we make provokes a roll of their eyes, or the advice is completely ignored. A patient of ours, in her early seventies, has learned how to achieve a wonderful relationship with her children, who are in their late forties. She tells me that her secret is very simple. She *listens* to her children more than she *talks*. She has a rule that she lives by; she never talks to any of her children about anything personal about the other siblings. She said that she learned this the hard way. Getting in between two siblings often results in a devastating aftermath, with several injured parties. She learned that direct communication between siblings, without her intervention, no matter how well intentioned, is the most productive course. She told me that her daughter called her the other night and opened the conversation with: "I am just venting right now. This requires no action or intervention on your part. I just want you to listen." She went on for twenty minutes recounting a situation between herself and her sibling. She listened and heard what her daughter said. At the end, she simply remarked, "I understand how you feel." Her daughter told her that at times like these it's wonderful to have her mother as a sounding board, knowing that whatever she tells her will not be communicated to anyone else. Another aspect of this 'listening' is that when the venting is over the anger subsides and the crisis situation looks a little more manageable to the adult child.

This parent-child interaction is yet another example of how much we learn from our patients, not only as clinicians but as parents ourselves.

4. Putting Stock in Close Bonds

We could not choose to study and understand adult children and their aging parents if we didn't first acknowledge how important these familial relationships are. Golish (2000) phrases it this way: "of the close relationships that people form in their lifetime, parent-child relationships are among the most enduring," (p.80). Umberson (1992) emphasizes that the relationships are essential to both parent and child and the bonds of close ties between them last all through the life course. The author stresses that the parent-child relationship is a permanent one that first evolves with strong dependency needs for survival of the child. As years elapse, and despite separations due to physical distance between parent and child, these bonds persist. The author believes, and we agree, that our society endorses the continuation of "social identity of parents and children," and the many shared values and social attitudes shape these relationships that much more.

We agree with the authors that these bonds are usually very strong yet the degree of closeness can take several forms, from being consistently close, to decreasing in closeness and even to a "roller coaster" kind of closeness (p.80). Golish is referring here to the kind of closeness that is represented by serial highs and lows. These changing states of closeness may be due to the events that occur in either the parent or the child's life (i.e. divorce, a move, unemployment or change of job). The author adds, however, that these states may also change due to ages of the family members involved. According to Golish, parent-adult child relationships strengthen over time and, in particular, the bonds of adult children and aging parent are more often strongest between mothers and their children. The author attributes this to societal and developmental causes, stating that girls, in general, are socialized to be the ones who build and nurture relationships. These findings are consistent with our practice experiences.

First, however, we must say that more women than men tend to seek counseling, so we have a larger sample of women from which to draw insights. Secondly, our clinical roster has always been comprised of a greater number of mothers searching for improvement in their family relationships and, more specifically, with their adult offspring. We give a lot of credit to these women as they often present with family backgrounds that did not teach or endorse the seeking out of mental health services for family problems. In fact, many of our senior patients explained to us that seeking therapy is something that they were the first in their families of origin to initiate. Some of our patients revealed that their adult child had sought treatment for problems or issues unrelated to the families of origin, and this served as an impetus for the older parent to consider counseling. They saw counseling as a new way of approaching a problematic situation that arose between family members. In almost all cases the senior parent was delighted to find that family counseling did have some merit and positive results could be seen, sometimes even after one session. This was especially true in those cases in which there was not much in the way of intimate feelings being openly communicated between family members.

Dana and Her Daughters

Dana was in her early seventies and her daughters Sandra and Sylvia were 47 and 45 respectively when she sought treatment with me because of her increasing distress about her relationship with her daughters. Dana, recently widowed, told me she had married at a young age because "I was pregnant"; however, she never regretted the choice of mate as "he was my one true soulmate." Having taken over her father's lucrative catering business when Dana was 42, life, in her own words, had been good to her. It was my patient's way of saying that she had earned a lot of money, making her lifestyle more than "comfortable". In addition, she invested well; therefore she did not want for anything. Her daughters, on the other hand, did not establish themselves in businesses or careers, and relied too heavily upon her generosity. Sandra dropped out of college during the first year and Sylvia completed a two-year degree in college and then bounced from one job to another, never being able to make ends meet. Although Dana had offered to take both of her daughters into the family business, both opted to continue trying to make it on their own, without much success. Dana bought Sylvia a car when she mentioned needing one and helped Sandra purchase an apartment once Sylvia married and could rely upon her husband to cover their monthly expenses.

In one of our early sessions Dana realized that she had adopted the 'savior' role in her daughters' lives. Instead of giving them the opportunity to work on their own issues or problems, she instinctually solved them by providing her daughters with the financial means as a solution, thereby keeping them dependent upon her. One can say that therapy can be a catalyst for insight that leads to change, however, in the case of Dana we are convinced that she arrived at her own epiphany when she realized that she was not helping her daughters, but rather enabling them to continue their dependency upon her. Although the process was very difficult for her to learn, she gradually withdrew from offering Sylvia and Sandra advice unless they directly asked. She learned this through role modeling and playing. There were a number of sessions in which Dana saw, for the first time, by assuming the role of one of her daughters, what they might have been thinking and feeling and it proved to be enlightening. Dana also began to examine her own lifestyle and became aware that she had diminished her support system through the years by concentrating all her time and effort on her two daughters. The friendships she once had suffered and, in some cases, became distant or nonexistent; therefore it wasn't easy for Dana to assert herself and communicate an interest in re-establishing ties. The patient learned how to approach these friends, sometimes via telephone and other times through letters or e-mail, with the help of a few sessions on assertiveness training. She had previously been frightened about the possibility of rejection and needed to practice what she would say and better understand how others may react to her tone and style of speaking. Dana made some real strides in this area and realized that the communication tools she learned had applications in other areas of her life, something she had not bargained for when she entered into therapy. Eventually, Dana started to strengthen the friendships she had maintained, and gained a hold of a few she had lost. She continued to cultivate her own interests and hobbies too. This 'letting go' was extremely beneficial, though we acknowledge difficult for all concerned; however, it provided the proper environment for personal growth and set the relationship between the three on a new and much more enriching plane.

Mother and Daughter Reunion

When Hilda came into therapy, at age 68, she said that whenever she has difficulty with her adult children, she kept remembering the admonition of her mother. When Hilda had her first child after a very difficult delivery, her mother stood by the bedside, stroked Hilda's tear-stained cheek and said, "That was the easy part, now you have to raise her!" Little did she know at the time how right her mother was! Hilda was to find out over the next several decades that 'parenting is forever'.

Having raised and married off her three children, she thought her job was done, and she could relax. Then came the grandchildren and the fun really began! Never realizing that she had the capacity to love anyone the way she did her grandchildren, she took to being a grandma with all her heart. Grandchildren offer the additional benefit of slowing down our sense of 'again' because they grow up so much faster than we grow old. Watching them in the family gives us the opportunity to reconnect with the years when we were young parents, just as raising our children allowed us to revisit our own childhoods. Author Jane Isay states in her own words: "I remember realizing, when I had my first child, that I could undo the mistakes I thought my parents had made with me. Like most people, I raised my children in light of what I remembered about what I liked and didn't like – doing the same or opposite, depending upon the situation," (Isay, 132).

Hilda entered therapy because she had a problem in her relationship with her youngest daughter, Stella. It seemed that over the years she found it increasingly difficult to form a relationship with her daughter. As a child Stella was a most demanding, jealous child, always presenting a challenge to her parents and daring them to love her, especially when she was most unlovable. According to accounts of my patient, Stella received a self-fulfilling prophesy to some extent, as Hilda had ambivalent feelings towards her throughout much of her childhood. In fact Hilda remarked, "I wish I had entered into therapy when she was little but I had the rest of my family to take care of and it wasn't easy for me." Hilda also felt that every time she looked at her adult daughter Stella, she still saw the bratty seven year old she had been, and as a result, their communications were tense and nonproductive.

Hilda didn't understand at first why she was so stuck in that cycle of seeing Stella as a young child, however, the insight work we did together created a clear picture for Hilda. It was almost like that light bulb that goes on after weakly flickering for many years. Hilda came to see that it was as if she were caught in a time warp. Hilda reported that when she had been a young child her beloved mother became ill and subsequently died a year later. She was forced to live with her stern, cold grandmother since her dad worked very long hours. Those were unhappy years for my patient. The feelings of abandonment by her mother, and then her father, kept getting replayed in some form as an adult and well into her role as a mother. The tapes of these memories from childhood got even more pronounced with the birth of her rejecting daughter and they continued to be replayed when the dynamics between them triggered old hurts for Hilda. Therapy helped Hilda separate herself from these traumatic memories of abandonment and it freed her to pursue a healthier relationship with Stella without the baggage from her past. It was a shame that Stella wasn't privy to the benefits of therapy that brought about an attitude change and a softening of the heart that her mother experienced.

Her daughter Stella, a professional in a highly esteemed position, was married to a successful lawyer and had two wonderful children. Since she lived several states away from her parents their primary means of communication was the telephone. Hilda found that her daughter was curt and impatient to the point of being rude whenever they talked on the phone. Hilda tried to question Stella about why she responded in such a disrespectful manner towards her, but Stella refused to discuss the situation. Hilda had a constant knot in her stomach and found herself feeling anxious and upset anytime she was on the phone with her daughter. The situation continued to accelerate until one day in therapy she broke down and cried uncontrollably. She said that she felt as if her daughter treated her like she was the child and Stella was the critical mother. She felt beaten up and defeated each time she and her daughter spoke.

In one of our sessions we discussed the fact that children are brought up to believe and understand that their parents' love is a constant. There are times they take advantage of, or test that 'constant love' with irreverent behavior, believing that no matter how they act, their parent will not abandon them or leave them without their love. Their parents' love represents a 'safe haven' for them and gives them free rein to 'act out', as teenagers do, in a rebellious fashion. They may say or do things to the parent that they would never do or say to another human being because they believe in the *'Guarantee'*, and would expect that their parents will love them always, no matter what.

Hilda, given her own history of abandonment by her own mother's death and her father's desertion at her grandmother's door, showered her daughter with everything that she was denied as a child. This included the *'Guarantee'* that she would never leave or stop loving her. On some level Hilda was resentful that her daughter was living the life that she wished she had lived. She would tell her daughter quite often, "You don't know how lucky you are; I wish I had the mother you have when I was your age." On some level, her daughter internalized the unspoken jealousy and resentment that was transmitted to her by her mother.

In therapy one day Hilda reported that she woke up in the middle of the night and decided she needed to write a letter to her daughter. "I had reached the end of my rope in the situation with Stella. I needed to put my feelings into a letter so that she would finally know how I felt without pussy-footing around. I would 'tell it like it is' for me," said Hilda, as she read the following letter:

> Dear Stella:
> In thinking about our volatile relationship and all the years of rudeness and disrespect you have subjected me to, I've decided to write this letter. I will not tolerate your insolence with me any more. I have endured your last tirade. Enjoy your life in good health, with good times and great pleasure from those you love; and please find someone else to use as your scapegoat. I am getting too old for this any more. You are my daughter and I will always love you, but I don't like you very much right now. Mom

Several weeks passed with no contact between the two women, although Stella called routinely to speak to her father. During our sessions, when Hilda became despondent about not hearing a word from her daughter about the letter, I asked her if she had to do it over again, would she still write the letter. "Yes," she replied, "I felt great relief after I wrote and sent the letter. I would do it again." I kept reassuring her that Stella read the letter and was absorbing it slowly.

During a phone conversation a week later Stella told her father that she received a letter from Hilda that made her feel very sad and hurt. She didn't say more and he didn't press her for more information. He only said that he read the letter and knew that Hilda was very upset as well. A few weeks later when Stella called Hilda answered the phone and decided to be cordial and asked how things were going with her daughter. Stella responded that she was busy redecorating the living room and was having great fun with the project. They chatted a bit and then her daughter nonchalantly said that she realized that sometimes her remarks can be cutting and she is trying to curb that tendency. Hilda said, "I understand," and after awhile the conversation ended pleasantly.

Hilda was overjoyed. "She heard what I said, and she's trying to change. I have hopes that something good will come from the letter I wrote." As the weeks passed, Hilda continued to bring reports of pleasant and satisfying conversations with her daughter. She no longer had a knot in her stomach when she heard her daughter's voice on the phone, and enjoyed the way the relationship was developing. "Maybe Stella needed a kick in the ass from me in order to treat me with civility and respect. Although it was out of character for me, I believe I advocated for myself by writing and sending that letter. I certainly feel that being frank, blunt and outspoken carried more weight than all the subtle, diplomatic pussy-footing around that she was used to receiving from me."

In retrospect, had Hilda read the letter to me beforehand, I would never have sanctioned her sending such a harsh letter to her daughter. However, in view of the positive outcome, in this case the patient may very well have known better than the therapist when it comes to communicating with their own child. It also is an example of how much I learn from my elderly patients.

Edward and Josephine had a father/daughter relationship that would meet the criteria for the roller coaster type of parent-child interaction mentioned above. Edward was 82 at the time he attended a brief period of therapy with me. The presenting problem was depression, secondary to grief over the loss of his second wife Millie. After attending a twelve-week bereavement group recommended by his good friend Charles, Edward agreed with his group counselor that he needed to continue with an individual therapist. This was the second time he lost a spouse, and both times the deaths were sudden.

The other members of Edward's bereavement group had begun, in the next to last session, to talk about ways to increase their social networks of friends and possibly start dating and Edward needed to talk much more about the loss of his 20-year marriage and the meaning his wife had for him. The unique aspect of this loss was that it brought back feelings related to the first spousal loss.

Following the death of his second spouse, Edward's social ties had diminished to his one friend Charles and what he described as an "up and down relationship" with his daughter Josephine. The patient's relationship with his daughter was negatively affected by Edward's choice of partner when he remarried after the death of his first wife Isabel (Josephine's biological mother). Nonetheless, Edward was the first to admit that his relationship with Josephine had suffered at other times in the past as well. He related, in therapy, that it was not easy for him to be demonstrative with his affection toward Josephine as both of his own parents had been strict and reserved raising him. When Josephine's mother unexpectedly died, Edward became closer to his daughter and was able to show his feelings more readily, something Josephine strongly needed. Edward couldn't fully explain what freed him up in the emotional sense, but he certainly recognized that he was enjoying the change. In the patient's view, "we bonded for the first time and the relationship grew stronger, which made us both happy." There was then an unfortunate change, after Edward married for the second time. Although her father was in his early sixties at the time, Josephine objected to the union and was insulted that Edward was choosing a mate outside of their religion.

Parent and child relationships afford both generations' very unique, special forms of socialization. The marriages of adult children bring with them in-law relationships and then grand-children, further strengthening the bonds formed in adult years of family relating. Maintaining strong family ties with parents is one way of lowering the risk of psychological distress for both, according to Umberson (1992). Difficulty arises, from our experience with therapeutic work, when one family member (the adult child or the aging parent) wants to maintain or even begin to form a close, strong emotional connection and the other doesn't or harbors uncertainty about resolving conflicts that were longstanding. There are so many myths that can be dismissed once a dialogue begins in therapy and each family member looks at their own perceptions about the relationship and challenges of what he or she thought the other felt. One of our patients explained it as the difference between saying, "this is what I said," and, "this is what I meant."

5. Communication Mechanics: Shifting Gears

Following many years of counseling seniors, from individual, group and family therapy perspectives and approaches, we decided to get together and discuss the need to write about some of these clinical experiences. A review of the literature further confirmed something we already suspected: the adult son or daughter's view is represented but the voice of the elderly parent is almost nonexistent. Many psychology professionals have shared their clinical and theoretical ideas about relationships between adult children and their aging parents, from the adult child's perspective. Numerous books and journal articles have been made available to help us better understand how an middle-aged son or daughter feels about caring for an older parent, whether the care takes place in a separate residence or the family members co-reside in either the parental home or the adult child's place of residence.

We dedicated a chapter to the adult child's perspective to indicate that we both respect and acknowledge the important role caretaking children adopt toward their parents. We are not minimizing the difficult struggles, ambivalent feelings, frustrations and sadness that often accompany the joy and bonding later in life between middle-aged offspring and their aging parents. What we are stressing here, however, is the need to include the unheard voice of the aging parent. This population has invaluable things to say and we have been fortunate to learn from them much of what we need to know in order to help strengthen intergenerational relating and bonding. We've reached a deeper understanding of how senior parents feel when they can no longer live alone and need to instead co-reside with an adult child. We better comprehend the way seniors feel toward their adult children when roles are reversed due to their need for care and help with decision making. As a result, we have come to appreciate how helpful a family intervention can be, as it provides a forum for the parent and adult child to openly discuss their unique concerns and, where needed, it offers mediation.

Dr. Moshe Vardy was a supervisor, mentor and friend to both of us. He was a big proponent of family therapy and often asked to meet family members, even if the identified patient did not ask for ongoing conjoint sessions. He felt that including the family members when obtaining personal history added a special contribution to the older person's treatment. Carol, our first author, has been running female support groups which have been comprised of mostly seniors. Often, the women talk about family relations with spouses and adult children and use the group as a sounding board for ideas regarding how to approach a conflict within the family. Barbara has done a great deal of bereavement counseling and therefore has encountered many seniors who have lost spouses, parents and adult children. They commonly come in for grief counseling but often decide to work on family issues with living relatives once the cloud of grief dissipates.

We have been providing therapeutic services to seniors for many years, with our patients' ages ranging from 65-85. The work is supportive in nature much of the time and, in the minority of cases, a more insight-oriented approach is applied. We have sometimes advocated a story-telling approach to therapy, as seniors like reminiscing about the past often through a sharing of family photos. Being able to tell their story is one way of connecting to another human being and, at the same time, connecting to their own past. The seniors simultaneously experience a sense of increased self-esteem as they realize, while narrating the story, that they have in fact accomplished a lot in their lives. A few of our case histories will reflect the cognitive behavioral approach to therapy, one that has been very successful with senior adults. It has helped these senior patients to question some of their patterns of thinking that may be faulty and even psychologically harmful to them. When a patient, for example, comes to his or her own realization that they are minimizing a need for help from the family or rationalizing why a senior adult residence is the best choice of lifestyle, cognitive behavioral therapy can play a major role in reframing a great deal of these thoughts, thus the patient's outlook and mood often changes as a result.

Having the parent's voice clearly stated, and conversations with adult children mediated, has also helped the adult son or daughter to learn new ways of approaching their parent. It has allowed for periods of reflection in which the adult child learns that he or she was assuming how their parent felt or even projecting what they may have felt if roles were reversed. Sometimes an aging parent has needed to tell their offspring that they truly do prefer their independence and want to continue living on their own, whether it is an adult residential facility or their own dwelling with attendant care. Adult children, after weighing the risks to health and safety, can help make a more informed decision with their parent, one that is realistic but also mutually satisfying to both. This can only happen when all the necessary conversations have taken place and all family members have been helped to see the true current status of things, along with being able to foresee possible consequences of living apart.

The following case history exemplifies one woman's struggle to be heard by her son. Upon entering therapy, Marcia bemoaned her relationship with her eldest son, Martin. He was a highly successful surgeon, married and the father of four children. He was distant from his family of origin and surrounded himself with his "upper-class neighbors in his exclusive area". At barbeques and social occasions he often seemed uncomfortable in the presence of his working class parents. He was, by her description, "a sarcastic man", who seemed to target her by belittling and embarrassing her. She disclosed that she had, on several occasions, talked to him of her feelings about his behavior towards her and asked why he treated her so poorly. His response was always, "Mom, you are too sensitive, you know I love you, that's just my sense of humor!" Marcia, as a result, began to doubt her own actions and she absorbed a persona of an incompetent mother who couldn't gain respect from her adult child. These feelings led to depression.

In our work together we examined the relationships she had within her nuclear family, the people she worked with and her friends. She had no trouble being assertive in most of her other relationships, but felt intimidated in her troubled relationship with Martin. She longed for his respect and kindness, which she felt were nonexistent.

We began a period of insight-oriented therapy because Marcia was on a quest to understand what she may have done to contribute to her communication roadblocks with her son. She had a sense that there was something in her family of origin but she wasn't able to make the connection without help. We reviewed Marcia's past history with each of her parents and some of her earlier memories as a child and young adult. During this period of exploration, Marcia started to recall more of her childhood and the memories helped her clearly see what she had been re-enacting in her family dynamics with her son.

Her father, from her memories of him, was "always poking fun at me in such a condescending way". He often said things that would make any young child cry or come close to crying, and, as a result, Marcia began to believe that she was despicable and unattractive. She took his teasing and criticism of her as true signs that she was unlovable and believed that if her own father didn't love her, how could anyone else?

She would seek out her mother's support and empathy at those times, but to no avail. Marcia vividly recalled how she felt in relation to her mother and she described the feeling of continuously walking around "all choked up," as though the feelings were lodged in her throat but had no escape. The message she internalized from her mother was that she should keep her feelings inside because she was supposed to be a mature young lady able to handle anything that came her way. So she continued this pattern of stifling her feelings throughout her childhood, believing that this was the correct way to function. The problem was that the squashing of her negative emotions created physical symptoms that were troubling to her.

In therapy we were able to utilize role play as a means of resolving the anxiety and despair that Martin's sarcasm provoked in her. After our insight work, it became clear to Marcia that Martin's mockery seemed to be just like her father's condescending criticism of her as a child.

We enacted scenarios about how she could field his barbs and still maintain her dignity. Utilizing events that had already occurred we discussed alternative responses she may have tried with Martin which would have maintained her dignity and reduced her anxiety. One occasion that came to her mind was a day she was visiting her son and daughter-in-law and their family. Her grandson had just gotten braces on his teeth and was showing how they worked with rubber bands. Offhandedly, Martin made a statement that when he was a child he needed braces but his parents didn't bring him to an orthodontist. I asked Marcia how the statement made her feel and she said, "I was mortified, embarrassed and shocked. It seemed to me that he was accusing me of neglecting his health. That was absolutely untrue! All my children visited the dentist every six months, and the dentist never mentioned a need for Martin to get braces. I would certainly have gotten them for him in a blink of the eye." I asked her what she did that day when Martin made such a nasty accusation, and she said, "I remember my eyes filled up with tears, I thought I would burst out crying. I stammered something like: 'You're a liar, that never happened', but I wish I could have calmly and clearly challenged him and redeemed myself in front of my grandchildren."

It seemed to me that Marcia was demoralized by her son just like she felt when her father teased her. She was afraid to unleash her anger at him and negated her feelings, as she had been so carefully taught by her mother. What she disclosed was the fear of having him shut her out of his and her grandchildren's lives. She felt she would rather swallow her anger to keep the peace than risk losing the relationship, however unsatisfactory, with her son.

Whenever she stifled her feelings and decided not to confront someone when they hurt her, she frequently suffered from headaches or pains in her neck and shoulders. I suggested that she begin keeping a journal of events such as the above, recording her feelings and reaction to the event. She understood that she was sabotaging her personal goals when she did not express her feelings and advocate for herself.

In the following weeks we discussed various ways for her to stand up for herself when she felt hurt. For several reasons we decided that e-mail was the perfect vehicle for communication between the two for the following reasons: it was not 'face to face confrontation'; e-mail can be modified and rewritten a hundred times before a person hits the 'send' button; and lastly, you can be sure that only the person you send it to can open it.

When Marcia came to my office in early May, she was upset at her son Martin's lack of attention to Mother's Day. In our session we spoke about the core reason for her hurt feelings and it came down to what she felt was a "lack of respect". What follows is her e-mail message to her son:

> I need to tell you that I feel angry at you for your insensitive treatment of me over the years. I have done nothing but love and support you and your family. I never forget a birthday, an anniversary or a holiday and have been more than generous not only materially, but also with my time and devotion to you

> and yours. In light of that, the lack of contact of any sort on Sunday, Mother's Day, from you or your family was hurtful. Ideally, I would have appreciated receiving cards from your family; an invitation to brunch, lunch, or coffee, anything to show that I am cared for. I also think that your children are old enough to recognize the importance of buying a card or making a phone call on Mother's Day. Children learn by example, and sadly, you have not been that example for them. Again, my son, I am angry at you and I hope you understand how I feel. Mom.

Martin got the e-mail and was able to comprehend his mother's feelings much clearer seeing them in print. He did not know how much his antagonistic, sarcastic attitude had been hurting his mom until he received the e-mail. Without ever mentioning the letter, he began trying to change his attitude towards her; at times slipping back into the old behavior, but on the whole, making a sincere effort to change.

To my surprise, several weeks later, Marcia came into treatment with an unusual request. She asked if she could invite Martin to our next session. She explained that her therapy would feel most complete if she had an opportunity, in the presence of her therapist, to explain to her son the insight she had gained regarding the pain associated to her relationship with her parents. The realization that she had carried over some of these negative dynamics into her present relationship with Martin was something she felt she needed to share with him in a safe environment. We were especially proud that she had the insight and the ability to come full circle and honor her feelings by asking for what she needed. By asking to invite Martin she independently completed the entire cycle of a successful therapeutic process.

Some of the dialogue between senior parent and adult child wouldn't have taken place if not for therapeutic intervention. The subject matter may be too delicate for one or both sides of the generational dyad. We have seen occasions in which the conversations or thoughts of the elderly parent have been suppressed for years and then finally emerged.

We have treated patients (adult children) who agreed to write letters to one or both parents as a cathartic effort and many of those letters invariably do not need to be sent. Instead, they are brought into a therapy session and discussed for their content and value as a catalyst in moving one's therapy along. We have also worked with senior patients who have received a 'letter of divorce' from one of their children, and the results are always devastating. In his book, "When Parents Hurt", by Joshua Coleman, Ph.D. (July 2007), examples are given by the author of letters of divorce, sent by young adults to middle-aged parents and they assertively indicate the child's wishes to be respected for his or her decision to sever ties with a parent. We respect their position. Although it is sad when an adult child feels there is no other choice but to permanently separate from a parent or set of parents, the cost to one's mental health to remain connected when there has been continuing abuse is more damaging.

One of our senior patients shared with us a letter from her daughter Heather, in which she talked about wanting distance from her mother after years of feeling criticized and cast aside. Heather's letter explained that she had, for many years, struggled with the thought of telling her mother that she no longer wanted to maintain communication because "it just has not worked." She went on to say: "I had hoped that therapy sessions together might help but they too crashed and burned. I just don't want to feel hurt and disappointed by her any longer nor do I want to do all the work trying to make our relationship better. I am not going to call or write to her anymore. I need to be distant; I need to feel healthy."

It has been our experience that some letters of divorce are based upon a child's life experience of abuse or neglect in their family of origin. Some of the abuse may have come in the form of verbal, physical, sexual or emotional abuse; or perhaps suffering from neglect or abandonment by a parent.

In some other cases, people who did everything in their power to be supportive, kind and loving to their children, still get a letter of divorce. Again, a passage from Joshua Coleman's book, "When Parents Hurt": "It is possible to be a devoted and conscientious parent and *still* have it go badly. You can do everything right and your child can *still* grow up and not want to have the kind of relationship with you that you always hoped you'd have... However, whether the parenting mistakes are subtle or serious, real or imagined, today's parents are completely confused by their children's accusations. They need guidance and support for themselves."

An Uncle's Abuse

Margie, a widow in her late eighties, came to my office complaining of a dark, overwhelming depression. For several weeks we concentrated on building trust and developing a therapeutic alliance by getting her present life situation out and onto the table. She revealed that she was widowed, had one child, a daughter, who was married and had a family of her own.

The problem began when her husband passed away several years ago. Out of the blue, her daughter sent her a 'divorce letter', enumerating incidents that proved beyond a shadow of a doubt that her daughter thought she was a terrible mother who was to blame for every unhappy moment that ever occurred in her life.

Margie described an incident that happened over forty-five years ago, when her daughter was seven years old. Her daughter seemed upset after a visit to her aunt and uncle's house (her sister and her husband lived two blocks away from them). Margie said that when she questioned her daughter, she revealed that her uncle had been doing awful things to her; things that made her feel dirty. Margie was devastated to think that something like this could happen in her family. Margie said she remembers going weak in the knees and felt as white as a sheet when her child continued to describe the acts of her uncle, the accursed pedophile. She said, "Of course, in those days, we didn't use terms like *pedophile* but now there is so much about sexual abuse of children in the newspapers that everyone knows the term." She spoke to her husband about what their daughter had told her. She said that he turned red as a beet with anger and raced to the cabinet where he kept his gun as he shouted, "I'll kill that bastard." Margie stood in front of the cabinet, blocking him from getting the gun. She spoke calmly and quietly and prevailed upon him to sit down and collect himself. She insisted that they both approach their daughter about the accusations before they took any action. Their daughter immediately confirmed what she had said, and added much more. Ashen, they went to her sister's house and confronted her brother-in-law. He admitted everything. They quickly severed all relations with her sister and her family.

After some time had passed they felt that their daughter was still troubled by the close proximity of her brother-in-law's family, so they insisted that her sister and brother-in-law take their children and leave town, or they would have him arrested. They moved to California shortly afterwards.

In our sessions Margie recalled forty-five years of many wonderful family occasions where they each garnered memories of loving family events. Their child's communion, schooling, dating, engagement, marriage and subsequent children were each marked with celebration and joy! She said that her husband died a happy man as he was surrounded by his loving family.

In our subsequent weekly sessions Margie spoke about how she grieved her husband's loss inconsolably. She proceeded to unfold a history of their loving relationship, beginning with the fact that they were childhood sweethearts who were married for sixty years, and neither of them ever looked at another person since she was thirteen and he was fourteen. They traveled extensively and cherished their home and family. He was her 'rock' throughout her adult life and she felt abandoned and empty without him beside her. She expressed anger at him for leaving her alone and she felt as if a piece of her was with him in the jar of ashes. She was at the lowest point of her life.

That was when her daughter sent her the letter of 'divorce' stating that she would have nothing to do with her. She made it very clear that she did not want to see her or speak to her. Then more letters came, accusing her of being a monster of a parent. Her daughter has several children, Margie's *grandchildren,* who were forbidden to keep in touch with her. The abject loneliness and helplessness she experienced were crippling. Holidays came and went without the warmth and love of a family celebration.

Margie said, "I have pleaded with my daughter on so many occasions to tell me why she hates me so much, but she ignored my calls and letters. I have asked her forgiveness many, many times for the hurts she says I caused her, to no avail." Concerning the sexual abuse her daughter suffered at her deceased brother-in-laws hands, Margie told her daughter many times that she did what she thought was best at the time, although it may not have been enough, and it may have been wrong. Margie stated over and over again that she was truly sorry for all the pain her daughter went through. "I often wish that I had had the courage to have my brother-in-law arrested at the time." Margie's only concern then was that in bringing the charges out into the open, her daughter would go through tremendous pressure, stress and anxiety. She was afraid that her daughter would be going through the humiliation, assault and violation all over again, publicly in the courts. She couldn't allow herself to create further pain for her daughter. In trying to protect her daughter, perhaps she was wrong. Looking back she thinks she *was* wrong. In Margie's own words, "That was over forty-five years ago and things were so different then." When she stopped speaking she cried softly and I sensed that Margie needed validation for her behavior so many years ago. Since I was convinced that she took the proper course of action at the time and was solely motivated by her need to protect her daughter, I agreed with her. I truly believed that in doing so, I supported the healthy part of her that needed to know she did the 'right thing'.

At a later session Margie described feeling broken apart at the way her life had developed. She was getting on in years, her health was diminished, and it was her fervent wish, before she died, to have her daughter, grandchildren and great-grandchildren in her home for a loving, happy holiday. Her greatest fear was that this was never to happen.

The sudden death of her beloved aunt brought Margie and her daughter together at the funeral. She hadn't seen her daughter in quite awhile and she looked older and more beautiful than she remembered. Her daughter was devastated, as she was, by her great-aunt's death. When her daughter saw her mother's ashen face she walked over and softly put her arms around her and kissed her. They both cried as Margie was wordlessly held and comforted. After the service her daughter asked if she could drive her home. "Of course," Margie said, "that would be wonderful."

They sat drinking hot tea in Margie's cozy kitchen when her daughter said, "I'm sorry, Mom. I know how close you were to Auntie, and how much you will miss her." Silently, she reached for her mother's hand and continued, "I think Auntie's death was a sign that 'time is fleeting' and I don't want to lose you before we have a chance to sweep away the wreckage of the past. That whole incident of my sexual abuse is behind me now, I've gotten on with my life, and I want so much to be a part of your life from now on. I know I've behaved irrationally towards you, but I was working with a therapist who made me believe that you were guilty of ruining my life. I believed her. I hope you can forgive me, Mom. I love you and want you in my life."

Margie said that although she was depressed and despondent during the period of time she experienced the loss of her daughter in her life, she held fast and never gave up hope. "Hope was the thread that held me together; hope and prayer." The approach to therapy, for this patient was existential in nature, an exploration of the meaning of the relationships Margie had with her aunt and spouse helped the patient understand what their losses meant to her and also gave Margie a definite sense that her therapist cared about her. Spillers (2007) states "an existential framework can offer one vantage point from which to understand a patient's inner, spiritual struggles with loss resolution," (p. 191). According to Margie: "Coming into treatment and being able to talk about the loss of my husband, then the loss of a relationship with my daughter, and the loss of my beloved aunt, and have you listen and understand my feelings, was a great help. My aunt's dying may have been the event that brought us together, but I always had faith that my daughter would be back in my life." Margie told me that the remnants of the severed relationship with her daughter are slowly being rewoven into a fabric, perhaps even stronger than the original weave.

They Love Me For My Money...

In another clinical case, Frank was 80 years old and quite alert, with his full memory intact. He lived alone since the passing of his wife, 14 years earlier. When he began treatment Frank was concerned that his children were always too busy to spend any quality time with him and only visited him on his birthday, Father's Day, and major holidays. Frank was lonely and felt distant from his children, and he claimed he couldn't understand the estrangement. He added that he was fortunate enough to have the means to always be very generous to them and continually gave them money.

Frank had three adult children, two sons and one daughter. All three were married with children. According to my patient

Frank, his children were always "buried in financial distress". Although that did seem to be the reality, what Frank didn't reveal at first was his authoritative and imposing attitude and posture toward his children. While he was very liberal about giving them money, there were always 'strings attached'. He wanted to have the last word about on what and how the money should be spent. For instance, Frank told them that they must send their children to Hebrew school and camp. When his children needed down payments to buy their homes, he told them what type of home would be best, and where they needed to buy their homes. Furthermore, our patient reminded his children that the homes ultimately belonged to him should he ever need the assets for his old age and healthcare.

This controlling attitude on the part of Frank was not only manifested in financial matters but in child-rearing opinions, purchasing of home improvements, where they should go on vacation, what type of car to drive and so on. This meddling in his children's lives often resulted in resentment and anger on the part of the adult child who may have felt manipulated and infantilized. Although Frank protested that giving his children money was the way he showed his love, this love was entirely conditional, and therefore may not have been perceived as love at all by his children.

In this case, the parent's voice needed to be reviewed, changed and softened if there was ever hope of a relationship developing between Frank and his children. The therapeutic road proved to be a rocky one indeed and a true challenge! It was difficult for Frank to comprehend that he was anything but a wise and benevolent father who did nothing but advise and help his children.

I asked Frank if he would like to ask any of his children to join him for a therapy session to enlist their help in improving the communication between them. Frank agreed that it might be a good idea and selected the son who he felt most alienated from to begin the process. Joe, his eldest son, agreed to attend a session although he wanted it "on the record" that he didn't believe in counseling. In the ensuing weeks Joe played an active role in Frank's therapy sessions. He was able to gently tell his father that he saw his 'generosity' as nothing more than thinly veiled controlling and manipulating of his children. Frank was visibly shaken when he heard Joe's statement. "I had no idea you felt that way, I never meant to be that way, I just wanted to help you guys," he said. When Frank told his son that he felt lonely and distant from his children, his son remarked that he felt as if his father revered his privacy and couldn't tolerate the chaos of getting together with the family. "You are wrong, Joe. Although I find it hard to ask for company from you and the family, I feel very isolated and I would welcome a visit from you," said Frank. "Well how can I know that if you don't tell me? We barely talk to each other when we are together anyway. I find it very hard to penetrate your hard shell, and I've all but given up having a relationship with you," said Joe.

Over the next several months, Frank brought his three children, individually, to help him break through his formerly impenetrable wall. Little by slowly, with each session, Frank was willing to accept the changes that his children, ever so gently, suggested. Our work is far from over but we can see tremendous growth in the family as a unit since the ongoing intervention began.

We have seen our patients exhibit a tremendous amount of courage and determination to evolve into softer more accepting people. It is tremendously hard to change, especially when you reach 'a certain age', but it is never too late to examine what doesn't work in your life and make the necessary adjustments and tweak that which needs to be tweaked. When our patients felt that their quality of life was not fulfilling or satisfying, they were not averse to looking within themselves, without pointing blame onto others, and correct the situation. That is why we refer to many of our patients as our "heroes"!

6. It Takes Two to Tango

We were not surprised to find that most of the articles and books in the available literature on the subject of intergenerational relationships were written from the adult child's perspective. Those authors talked about the 'sandwich generation' and the caretaking role of the middle-aged son or daughter of an older parent. They further elaborated on the ambivalent feelings many adult children have and the conflicts they experience communicating with their parents as they grow further into adult years. We concluded that, although it is not our main focus, the adult child's viewpoint should not be neglected in a book on this topic, and therefore we will provide a summary about the common themes adult children feel when interacting and taking care of their senior parents.

The theme that arises most commonly when reviewing what has been written over the past decade concerning adult children is their caretaking role with their elderly parent and sometimes both parents. In many cases, it seems the adult child initiates that the older parent move in with them, and in other situations the aging parent might ask their son or daughter to help with their care. That could translate into moving into one or the other person's residence, or it could mean that the adult child will make regular visits to his or her parent to check on the status of their parent's health and safety.

In a study conducted by Silverstein & Bengston (1994), an investigation was done to see whether social support from adult children improves the psychological well-being of elderly parents. The authors ask whether quality of life for elderly parents is contingent upon the quality of intergenerational relationships. It has been argued that families in post-modern society have become less important for satisfying basic social needs of older relatives because intergenerational families have become less socially and economically interdependent. Older people, in this view, are more likely than ever before to be isolated from their families, especially from adult children, causing feelings of alienation and psychological distress. In our work with the elderly, we find the opposite to be true. The psychological health of the elderly patients is in direct proportion to the amount of filial response to their situation. Two of the most prevalent life events causing stress in old age are the death of a spouse and the loss of physical health. It is well documented that the widowed may also experience chronic stress related to loss of income, relocation and the transition to a new social status and lifestyle, according to Silverstein & Bengston (1994). The authors point out that it is likely that acute and chronic stressors operate jointly to dampen feelings of well-being among the widowed.

Donofrio & Sheehan (2001) use a term "filial maturity" to describe a developmental task in which adult children come to realize that their parents have limitations due to aging and they (the adult son or daughter) need to assume responsibility. The authors explain that it becomes necessary for the adult child to change the pattern of relating they once had with a parent, to include a realistic view of the mother or father's strengths and weaknesses, otherwise the adult son or daughter will become overly stressed and anxious watching the deterioration in a parent's health.

Edna and Michelle

One of our clinical cases is that of Michelle and her mother Edna. Michelle, at the time family counseling began, was a 55-year-old single female who never married. Her mother Edna was 78 years old when Michelle insisted she move into her home. Michelle owned her own home as she was a successful corporate executive. She explained to her mother that she (Michelle) had no other responsibilities other than her work therefore assisting in the care of her mother would be feasible. According to Michelle, the new living arrangement became necessary as every time she visited her mom, she noticed something that left her feeling worried. One time it was a medication bottle that held the same number of remaining pills for days, and another time, it was the fact that Edna started talking about speaking to her older sister Ellen who had actually died 5 years prior to that. Michelle realized that her mom would need help during the day, while she was at work, and she had the means to hire a private homecare worker for a Monday through Friday, 9 a.m. to 7 p.m. shift. The schedule seemed to be working out just fine until one day several months after Edna moved in with Michelle and the homecare worker was an hour late. Michelle stated: "If only I didn't go to the business meeting first thing in the morning, I may have been able to prevent the accident." Edna took a fall in the bathroom and sustained an injury to her right shoulder, which necessitated surgery. Michelle was left with a lot of guilt feelings, but what was not expected was that Edna slipped into a clinical depression during her hospital stay of six days. A social worker came to see Edna in the hospital and suggested to Michelle that she encourage her mother to continue with the social service home visits, which Michelle concurred would be absolutely needed for part of her mother's recovery. Medicare allowed several visits by a social worker and she met with Edna for the majority of the sessions and also with Michelle jointly and alone. The social worker, once the services through Medicare were exhausted, suggested the family seek further mental health services privately. Once Edna was mobile again, Michelle brought her mother to my office for the next eight months and it was Edna who asked that her daughter be present at the sessions. It seemed she had more clarity when Michelle was there to address issues at home or provide history about Edna.

One of the family issues that surfaced was Edna's feeling that she wanted to be included more in the decisions made about her health and physical care. While she knew Michelle had only the best intentions, there were times in which "I didn't feel I was being asked, but rather that I was being told what to do." According to Johnson (2005), the absence of talking about each other's needs, emotions and wants can have a dramatically negative impact on the relationship between a senior parent and his or her adult child. The author believes, and we concur, that one of the tasks of the clinician is to make sure that the family is encouraged to include all immediate members in the process of making decisions. Johnson explains that "effective communication can make a great difference in the parent's acceptance of increasing dependence upon others and may eliminate some anxiety and fear on the child's part regarding what the best decisions may be," (p. 95). Of course, there can be a limit to that involvement if the aging parent has an organic basis for memory loss (i.e. in such cases as early dementia). In the above case, Michelle agreed to listen to her mother's request to be heard, but when she felt that Edna's health might be compromised she followed her own instincts and gently rejected the suggestion. For an example, Edna told her daughter that she wanted to discontinue the services of the day care aide that provided full-time care. Upon investigation, Michelle discovered that Edna had been slipping in and out of lucidity and had accused the aide of hiding her shoes. As days passed Edna had become increasingly angry and belligerent towards the aide and wanted her gone. Michelle intervened by telling her mother that she would make sure that the aide would not hide her shoes again, but she could not let her go. Her mother seemed content that her daughter would "take care of the situation". This vignette illustrates the importance of having the caretaker daughter hear her mother's voice and respond in a way that satisfies her mother's need to be heard, without giving in to her request.

My Mother, My Child

There may come a time in the adult child's life when their strong, independent, highly intelligent parent declines with age. This is a naturally occurring phenomenon in many people's lives and it is usually extremely difficult for the adult child to accept. As a result they may adopt the stance of denial, or refusal to admit that their parent can fall prey to something as dreadful as dementia, for instance.

Such is the case with my patient who lived two hours away from her widowed mother. For years after her father's death she spoke to her mother several times a week and visited her monthly, usually with her younger sister. They would take the two hour trip together, spend the weekend with Mom, go shopping with her, help her shop for groceries and enjoy the entire experience.

Soon their mother complained about her checkbook being "off", and on closer inspection, the sisters found that their mother had been sending checks in duplicate to all the utility, phone, and rental companies. They decided to visit every other week, and handle the checkbook for her, much to their mother's protestations and angry words. She kept repeating, "I am not addle-brained, I can do this," but it was clear that she could not. The progression became more rapid. Calls came from her mom's neighbor saying that her memory was slipping and could no longer play the treasured games of mah-jongg or canasta, because after fifty years of playing she forgot how. This alone decimated the socially interactive circle she had been happily engaged in for many years. They found that her loneliness and isolation caused her to be depressed and sad. She would call my patient at her office eight or nine times a day, forgetting she made the previous seven or eight calls.

By now the sisters came to visit every weekend. They continued to shop and cook meals for their mother, labeling each package with "eat this for lunch", "this is for dinner", and so on. When they returned the following weekend, they noticed uneaten, spoiled food in the refrigerator, medication not taken, and a marked decrease in their mother's personal hygiene. Their denial had been shaken. Mom was at risk living alone. They decided that she needed to live with my patient. The process was debilitating and demoralizing for all of them. Their mom's spirit was broken; she did not want to give up her home, her life, her independence, and yet even she knew on some level that she could no longer stay alone. With defiance and anger she agreed to the transition, and they moved their mother to my patient's home, which she shared with her husband.

Since both my patient and her husband went to work each morning, they suggested to mom that they would get a companion for a few hours during the day to keep her company. She vehemently denied the suggestion, so they played a 'wait and see game'. The first few weeks were blessedly uneventful, with mom spending her days reading and watching TV. Since it was spring, mom decided to take a walk each morning. Soon, their neighbor reported finding their mom crying on the corner, not knowing where she was. Their neighbor gently brought her back to the house, and calmed her down.

At my suggestion during our sessions, I asked that my patient keep a journal of her feelings during this tense, emotion-laden time. What follows is a composite of several entries:

> She was being obstinate as she told me she won't change from her nightgown to her street clothes. I raised my voice, almost ordering her to change and she yelled back "no" several times and wouldn't even look at me. In part, it sounded like a mini temper tantrum and I could envision her stomping her feet if this exchange were to go on any longer. It made me think of what it must have sounded like when I was a child refusing to get out of bed or take a bath. I felt frustrated, impatient and angry. I wanted her to cooperate. I wanted her to do what I said. Somehow, I felt as if her being dressed properly was a reflection on me. I know that parents feel that way, and they

continue to feel that way even when their children are adults, but here I was instructing my 83-year-old mother about appropriate behavior! I yelled at her, or maybe I raised my voice several times. I felt driven to state my position but, at the same time, I felt ridiculous in asking. I also felt a pang of guilt. After all, I can't say I remember being talked to the way I spoke to my mother that day. My tone was probably authoritative and had a hint of sounding condescending."

"Mom, people are coming over. The least you could do is get dressed and comb your hair," I implored. The posture I adopted was supposed to be convincing, since the "people" coming over were not family, but instead were new friends. Was I thinking, somewhere in the back of my mind, that she would embarrass me? It sounds awful but I must admit it is certainly feasible. Of course, that doesn't detract from the fact I have been thinking as of late that she is depressed and that also makes me feel angry. Here she is, a mother who knows her child more than 50 years, and she doesn't take my advice. There have been times that I have told her she is depressed and it sounds, in retrospect, like I am accusing her of something. Does she have faith that I even know what I am talking about when I make these claims about knowing when someone is depressed?

Why do I still need her approval anyway, and why will I go to these lengths to get it? I guess that is the most disturbing part of all. I recall leaving the house for a short while after we argued about her getting dressed. When I came back, she was in the process of putting on some casual clothes and it looked like she was struggling with closing buttons on her blouse. I felt sad, angry at myself now and also a bit relieved at the same time. I was going to have my way, I won the battle and she was finally listening to me, but now the stakes felt so different. I won by being a bully perhaps. Did it mean that my mother felt intimidated by me? Had she come to agree that

> getting dressed to receive guests was the right way to go after all? Was I teaching her values or pushing her around? I complimented her on how she looked. I also realized that I hadn't seen my mother dressed in clothes in a long time. Maybe I rationalized it and told myself that "it is good for her". I'm not sure. My mother came out of her bedroom and socialized with company. In the past, she had stayed isolated in her room until people left our home, watching TV. I should have told her that I was sorry for raising my voice at her as I am sure it affected her. In my recollection of the earlier conversation, she stuck to her guns and refused to get dressed but I can vaguely recall that she was noticing my facial expression and was upset that I was displeased. I always said she was good at reading faces, even with her severe visual impairment. She also has a selfless way about her, so most likely she got dressed to please me. I don't think I am as selfless as she is with my children but I do set limits with them more than she did. Should I be setting limits with her? That's the more pressing question.

The strong emotions, the ambivalence and the guilt shared in the journal entry above are very natural and common expressions of adult children who are smack in the middle of taking care of an aging parent with dementia; a role that they did not chose to play, a role in which they feel totally inadequate and unprepared to handle. We have known many caretaking sons and daughters who feel angry at themselves for not having more patience in dealing with this disease in a parent and others who feel it is too difficult to admit to angry feelings toward their parent for the many sacrifices they have had to make. Seeing a therapist each week has given this woman in the above scenario (and others) a chance to vent her feelings, neutralize her emotions and work on ways to continue the challenging, arduous job that has become hers.

7. Tiptoe Through the Turmoil

Luescher and Pillemer (1998) state that intergenerational relationships have been studied over the course of three decades, between the 60's and 90's. These authors believe that "intergenerational relations generate ambivalence," and we feel it is very important to address this concept since we have spoken to many adult children and aging parents who have expressed strong mixed emotions toward one another (p.414). This research team further defines "intergenerational ambivalence" as "contradictions in relationships between parents and adult offspring that cannot be reconciled," (p. 416). These contradictions can occur at a level of social structure or at a subjective level. We beg to differ and instead hold the belief that some of this ambivalence can be worked out with the help of supportive counseling, combined with insight work with the parent individually and also with family work.

According to Luescher and Pillemer, the sociological kind of ambivalence encompasses norms and social roles that contradict each other, and the subjective level implies contradictions in thoughts, feelings and motivations. One type of ambivalence identified by the authors is dependence versus autonomy. On both sides, there is a conflict between wanting to be independent and simultaneously wanting nurturance, assistance and support. Luescher and Pillemer talk about the same kind of ambivalence we found in many mother-adult daughter dyads, in which the mother wants to live with her adult child yet also feels the loss of her autonomy as she gives up independent living. Another kind of ambivalence rears its ugly head when the mother and daughter have a close bond, make daily contact or even live with one another, as in our case of Beth and her daughter Sheila. However, there is also a stress and tension felt by both parent and adult child, particularly when the parent does not approve of the lifestyle choices made by her daughter.

Beth came to see me, at the age of 82, as in her own words: she needed to "talk about how my daughter and I are managing living together again, after 30 years". When Beth was 52, her daughter Sheila went off to college in another state. Upon graduation, she became a marketing research assistant and married a salesman whom she met at her company. Their marriage lasted 17 years; they had no children and Sheila then remained single due to trust issues, following her husband's repeated infidelity.

Beth's daughter came to visit on a regular basis once her father passed away. According to Beth, Sheila became aware that her mother needed daily help once she turned 81. Her mobility was restricted after two serious falls, resulting in hip replacements and she had a serious hearing impairment as well.

Initially, Beth resisted the idea of moving in with Sheila. She had been living alone for one year and, in her estimation, was faring well, and having various friends check in on her almost daily. Her adult community provided a service in which Beth could get all her needs met at the neighboring stores for a minimal price, but "my daughter knew I slept alone at night and that made her nervous." Beth explained that she appreciated that her daughter recognized a need for them to live together. "There were too many physical problems," she said, "and my daughter refused to consider that I live alone or in assisted living." Beth never wanted to be placed in a facility as she recalled how much her own father hated that kind of living arrangement. Sheila was in total agreement that family members should be there for one another, and although Beth would have lived alone, had Sheila not suggested sharing a place together, she eventually came to see it was not the most realistic choice.

After several conversations with her daughter, Beth stated she would move in with Sheila. At that time, both had been living in the same state which made the move a bit easier. Beth felt the situation was "sweet and sour". On the one hand, it was a blessing to live with her daughter and it reduced the fear that an older parent has about living alone and caring for oneself, however, there is a "price to pay" too. Beth felt she had given up her own apartment, in an adult community that she used to love, where her friends dwelled and she was comfortable with her daily routine. Beth explained that it is not just the giving up of independence and consistent friendships, but also the loss of material items (furniture and personal belongings) that could not be accommodated in a shared residence.

The patient expressed that it is not easy when she and her daughter, "don't see eye to eye." In those moments, she realized that her daughter is "a younger, more educated woman with different ideas and opinions," however, certain decisions she makes disturb Beth and "it is hard to look away." Stephen A. Bly, in his book, "Once a Parent, Always a Parent", states that in situations such as Beth's our roles will certainly change and vary with our children's ages and circumstances, but we will always be parents, and our job is never finished. However, discussions with adult children which may have ended with, "I'm your mother and I said so," when they were nine years old, will not work when your child, like Sheila, is in her fifties. At some point, the boundary lines change and parents need to accept the fact that their children are adults, and should be considered as a peers or contemporaries.

One of the items Beth wanted to discuss was her daughter's choice of dating partners. It seemed that Beth certainly endorsed the idea of a partner for her daughter and recognized that Sheila was an adult, entitled to choose a man she is attracted to, but "then there was Robert". He was also divorced and had been dating Sheila for six months, at which time Beth sized him up to be "lazy, inconsiderate and unreliable." After Robert, there was Steve and each time they had a date he came directly from his job, as an auto mechanic, "the kind that doesn't wash up after a day's work." I knew after hearing the first two stories that Beth needed to place some of the therapeutic concentration on balancing her concern for her daughter's partner choice with an appropriate amount of involvement in her personal life, otherwise resentment would naturally build, since Sheila wanted and needed the privacy that adult children need.

In one of our individual sessions, Beth and I discussed the parallel between her and her daughter. Each of them, in different ways, needed more personal space and independence. Beth was able to identify with her daughter's feelings when I engaged her in role playing. In the process we role modeled various scenarios of mother-daughter interactions. However, she found it difficult to actually confront her daughter in person. Beth couldn't envision how she would transfer what she learned about communication in our sessions to the reality of a face to face talk with Sheila. It took a few more sessions for Beth to come to the realization that parenting, to her, meant being liked by her daughter. Beth recalled many years, when Sheila was growing up, in which Beth was unable to set boundaries with her daughter or say "no" in general, for fear that Sheila would resent her. This was a revelation for Beth and she easily tied in some of the current behaviors as an extension of the same mentality: "I wanted to keep everything nice between us."

One of the essential, concrete ideas that we discussed repeatedly in our sessions was: "Unsolicited advice is often regarded as criticism." Beth became increasingly aware of how her unsolicited advice about her daughter's choice of friends was shunned and often provoked anger and resentment in her daughter. Beth needed to realize that she was no longer the mother of a twelve-year-old daughter who had to listen to her mother. She found that moving back with her daughter at this stage of both their lives meant she had to relinquish her role of 'mother with absolute power' that she had when Sheila was a child. The new role she needed to adopt was the one of sharing a house with her daughter on a peer level relationship. After all, they were both adults, she lived in her daughter's home, and to coexist within a harmonious relationship she needed to become more flexible and accepting of her daughter.

In one of our sessions Beth recalled recently having several dreams about her daughter, and was surprised to disclose that in her dreams her daughter was always a child. She described the dreams to me as very pleasant, touching moments between a mother and her child, Beth and Sheila. When we spoke about her dreams in depth, she realized that she was happiest at that time in her life. She was the loving, all-knowing wise mother, and Sheila was the dutiful child. Beth realized that it was during that time that she was able to have full control of everything her child did. It made her feel proud, capable and fulfilled. These feelings were in contrast to the feelings she experienced at this point of her life, in her relationship with Sheila.

We had our work cut out for us; we needed to find that delicate balance between sharing her feelings with Sheila without giving unsolicited advice, rolling her eyes and giving disapproving looks when she was disappointed with her daughter's choices. She wanted to internalize the fact that Sheila was an adult, fully capable of making reasonable choices. In time, she found that the more she treated her daughter as an equal, the more her child gradually began to come to her for counsel.

In time, it got easier for Beth to embrace the idea of having a conversation with her daughter about changes in their relationship. Before long Beth called to ask for an earlier appointment than the one scheduled in order to relate that she and Sheila talked over dinner and found a happy medium from which to continue their adult parent-child relationship.

Becoming a roommate with your daughter after thirty years of separation can be difficult and challenging at best, but with the continuing guidance and support Beth is garnering in therapy, it is no longer the impossible dream it had once been.

Wilson, Shuey & Elder (2003) discuss the greater likelihood

that adult daughters will be caring for their elderly parent as "bonds between mothers and daughters tend to be the strongest and most enduring of filial ties and women have the most consistent, direct contact with other generations," (P1057). The authors also indicate that, from their research on these relationships, this greater dependency upon daughters places parents and their adult offspring at greater risk for ambivalent feelings and a need to renegotiate the roles of power in the relationship. The authors emphasize the added stress of a daughter caretaking her senior mother or father while trying to juggle her family responsibilities with her own children and career. As we see from our stories about our own patients, sometimes this juggling act occurs all under the same roof, further complicating matters on a daily basis at times. Johnson (2005) speaks of the problems of the daughter who feels unappreciated by the older parent she is taking care of. Of course, it is conceivable that these offspring also feel relief knowing that on one hand they are taking care of their parent, but on the other hand they feel taken for granted, resentful or hurt when the parent doesn't acknowledge their care and support. Thus we face yet another kind of intergenerational ambivalence.

According to Montoro (1994) the key factor is whether the adult child and aging parent interact in a manner that is cooperative or competitive. If their interactions are competitive, then it behooves the clinician/researcher to uncover patterns that may exist preventing these family members from managing conflicts. One might ask at this juncture, what are the middle-aged adults and their aging parents having conflicts about? Clarke, Preston, Raksin & Bengston (1999) discovered common themes involving communication and style of interaction between aging parents and their offspring. This research group discovered that older parents and their adult children disagree over personal habits and choices, practices in raising children, politics, religion, ideology, work habits and ways of handling a household. As for the latter, one can only imagine how tense living together can become if there are differing ways of managing that household, usually one in which the adult child is the woman or man of the house. Johnson (2005) stresses the importance of communication between parent and adult child, especially when there is increased dependency on the part of the parent. The author takes this concept to a whole new level when she emphasizes the possibility that poor communication can have a rippling effect, in that other family members are impacted negatively as well. According to Johnson, the family members need to be a part of the decision-making process and should be included in family sessions regarding the older parent where appropriate.

Tim was now with the second woman in his life and he was in his early seventies. He felt that he had finally found the right partner in Diane, a woman who loved and respected him for the good person that he was. Just when he was close to giving up on love of women, a good friend introduced him to the woman who "changed my life in many ways." Tim added, "If only my relationship with my son Thomas was less problematic."

His first wife Iris had betrayed him. She was having an affair with the neighbor's husband, after having borne Tim two children. Tim was devastated by this betrayal. It was the support of his oldest daughter Gabrielle that helped him through the subsequent period of separation, and ultimately divorce. When Iris announced in a heartless manner, "I am going to live with my boyfriend," Tim gave Iris the house and just about anything else she wanted. It was his priority that she have a decent home with which to raise their children, since she was designated the custodial parent.

We met when he came to see me with his second wife. He told me that his marriage was being negatively affected by the chaos between him and his 40-year-old son Thomas. Marital sessions were implemented first and it was quickly revealed that Diane resented the interactions between Tim and his son. According to

Diane, Tim had these "screaming matches with his son Thomas; like a constant competition." Tim agreed with his wife that, now in his latter years, "My son wants to rule over me and I won't have it." He described several incidents in which Thomas tried to exert too much control over his life and it left him feeling frustrated, irritated and sometimes enraged. Since Diane was a social worker, she felt the need to intervene, as though "I was hooking right into crisis intervention mode," but according to both of my patients, all her efforts unfortunately failed. Diane tried getting Tim to read self-help books and since he was an avid reader with an interest in psychology, he complied. No outside resource prepared him to successfully communicate his needs to his overbearing son. I explored what the issues were and Tim enumerated several. He told me that his son wanted him to retire from his part-time job as a shoe salesman, despite the fact that Tim enjoyed the social component of being employed and also felt a sense of belonging to the community of semi-retired people. Since Tim had a mild heart attack the proceeding year Tim could empathize with his son's concern for his health and level of stress. However, both he and his doctors had agreed that he could continue working part-time and going for quarterly check-ups. According to Tim, Thomas wanted his dad to move close to his sister, so that he wouldn't make the drive to see his grandchildren, and Gabrielle could look after him when Diane was not home. In fact, "He tried to bully me into giving up driving altogether." Tim explained, in an upset, exasperated tone, that he wouldn't drive if he didn't feel capable. The relationship between Tim and his adult son took a worse turn when Thomas decided to call Tim's doctor to get test results. Tim explained that he felt infantilized by this behavior and he lost his temper when he spoke to his son about it.

I explored the relationships Tim felt he had with his children while in his first marriage. They were quite different from what they evolved into, once Tim and Iris divorced. Tim felt that, from the outset of the divorce, his son outwardly displayed their anger and disappointment towards Tim. My patient explained that he believed this was due to the fact that "my son was closer to me and couldn't easily express his emotions to his mother." Now, as an adult, Thomas had resolved a great deal of his angry feelings in his own therapy, but what remained for Tim was a posture Thomas adopted toward him that Tim felt was punitive and controlling. The additional stress Tim was feeling related to his disappointment that Thomas, unlike his daughter, never made much of an attempt to foster a positive relationship with him.

I saw Tim individually for a few months and he took to therapy like a fish to water. A good part of our work together revolved around educating Tim about reintegrated families and the complexities of the dynamics between adult children and their aging parents as well as stepparents and adult stepchildren. The stepfamily is new water to most and often people find themselves doggy paddling for some time before settling into a comfortable family milieu.

The approach that was helpful in our therapy was a cognitive behavioral one, better known as CBT. According to several authors, this kind of therapeutic technique is quite effective with older folks (Satre, Knight & David, 2006; Crowther & Zeiss, 1999). We felt in Tim's case that CBT would help him identify areas of strength, while also, in a team approach between therapist and patient, set realistic goals for achieving harmony with his son Thomas. One of the goals agreed upon by patient and therapist was for Tim to be able to put in writing his feelings toward his son. In particular, Tim would list all the things he wanted to address about their relationship. He wouldn't approach his son about these things but instead he would bring the list into a therapy session and we would review it. Tim could then decide what to share with Thomas and what to discard. He even set aside a 'D' folder in his computer, in which he kept 'Discarded' lists, in case he wanted to refer back to them at some later point.

In the past Tim thought that he had to tell his son everything or he wasn't being honest or having an open relationship with him. This 'all or nothing' thinking had gotten Tim into trouble and a therapeutic approach challenging the irrational thinking seemed to assist Tim a great deal.

After two weeks of our reviewing Tim's lists, we decided that it would be beneficial if his son was invited to a therapy session. When he called his son Tim made it clear that his attending would aid in Tim's therapy and would be helpful to him in communicating his feelings. He made it very clear that this was not going to be a 'let's fix Thomas' session. Thomas agreed and did come to one session. When they came into my office I was surprised to see that they were laughing and Tim had his arm around Thomas' shoulder, projecting camaraderie. It was revealed to me at a later date that the two met for dinner before our appointment and some bonding occurred at the dinner table.

The session was quite astounding. Tim shared some of the frustration and anxiety he felt as he aged, and Thomas listened very intently. When Tim described his desire to get closer to his son, Thomas declared that this was his wish as well. They both agreed to a conjoint visit once a month. One of their mutual goals would be to try to put the past behind them and concentrate on the future.

Our therapeutic work has confirmed the point made by Clarke, et al (1999), that older parents and their adult children often complain about communication being "strained or nonexistent," (p.265). The reader will note that in a few of our stories, the older parent wanted more communication with their son(s) or daughter(s) and some were uncomfortable (i.e. afraid) to confront their adult children, or ask for more contact, for fear of causing further estrangement. Our therapeutic work with such patients of older years entailed helping them see the grey area. The communication with their adult sons and daughters did not always have to be all or nothing, black or white. Instead, these senior patients learned new ways of approaching their adult children without necessarily coming across as overbearing, controlling or critical. Sometimes this involved a different medium of expressing feelings, such as letters instead of phone calls or listening in an attentive, guided fashion instead of asking questions that could be perceived as criticism.

David had been thinking of seeing a therapist at least six months before he actually made the appointment. He explained that he was embarrassed to talk about the problems he was experiencing. David told me that now at his ripe old age of 87 he wished his life would feel less complicated. According to David, his daughter Cathy "almost cut me out of her life." About one year ago, Cathy revealed to my patient that she had been sexually abused by her paternal grandfather. David described feeling like he was "hit in the stomach with a bowling ball" when Cathy shared a memory of her grandfather's cold hand reaching under her clothes to fondle her on those Saturday nights when he watched Cathy and her younger brother. On those weekend nights, David and his spouse went out with other couples for the evening. In response to his daughter's revelations, David told me, "It can't be true," and he told his daughter the very same thing. He later came to realize that it was his insistence that Cathy falsely remembered events from childhood that caused them to have arguments which eventually escalated to a falling out last year. According to David, his daughter only told him about the sexual abuse memories, not her mother. "My daughter feels that telling her mother would kill her on the spot," David stated. "It's OK, though, to tell me?" David asked rhetorically. The patient wanted me to understand that, for him, the anguish is even more painful, as Cathy was pointing to his father as the perpetrator.

In our therapy sessions, David recounted the past year of his severed relationship with Cathy as he struggled with ambivalent feelings and thoughts. On the one hand, he wanted to believe his daughter, which made him feel profoundly sad, but on the other hand, he couldn't believe his daughter, as it raised feelings of anger and hatred toward his father that seemed impossible to handle. The past year was especially difficult and lonely for David because since Cathy's disclosure, "It seemed as if a chasm had developed, which was impossible to cross." He missed the closeness that they had shared before her revelation and he missed seeing her and knowing that she was safe. He felt very sad and depressed at his loss, the loss of her company and the fact that he felt he had been responsible for cutting off the relationship by not believing her story. My patient tearfully recalled the many family occasions and holidays in which he did not see his daughter and the countless times he called other family members to see if she was alright, since Cathy wouldn't return his calls.

David knew that, with his father gone, he would never have the chance to confront him and he regrets that he did confront his daughter. In fact, he shared with me that upon first hearing Cathy's secret, he raised his voice in disbelief and then condemned her for wrongly accusing her grandfather. David also struggled with the possible notion that, in the last years of his life, because of his rejection of her accusation, he would have little or no contact with the person who meant the most to him, Cathy. Therapy revealed that David's marriage had been tumultuous for many years, but "my daughter always brought me joy to off-set that pain." He added that he had the gut feeling his father also had a stormy marriage and may have wanted a divorce at one point but instead stayed "for the sake of the children". David said he never would have thought that his father was behaving in an inappropriate manner with a grandchild. In fact, he said, "It was the furthest thing from my mind." After the death of her grandfather, and near her 50th birthday, Cathy approached David with her story she had kept buried for many years. He was outraged that she could make such accusations about the father he loved all his life. He shared with me that the pain he felt at the mere chance she was telling the truth was even greater.

Ambivalence was what he felt. David wanted to believe that his precious child, and only daughter, had not been sexually touched at the age of 10, by her grandfather, his father, yet if she was, David wondered why she allowed it to continue until she was thirteen years old. These ambivalent feelings, and the ramifications they brought with them, forced David to choose not to believe it actually happened. One day, about a month or two after starting treatment with me, he called Cathy and asked her over for tea. They talked about the past, those Saturday nights when Cathy was in her grandfather's care and they reviewed what Cathy believed occurred and the reason it continued. Cathy explained to her father that she felt loved by her grandfather, even when he was touching her and bringing her to orgasm, yet somehow she simultaneously knew that this behavior was not acceptable and should not be made public, especially to the rest of the family.

David wanted to know why Cathy made him privy to her secret last year. What was to be gained, especially so many years later? When he asked Cathy, she had only one justification, and that was a need for some kind of closure. David was her father and the closest living relative to her grandfather and she needed someone to know and someone to subsequently believe her. There finally came a time when David believed Cathy. The catalyst was a joint session in which each of them openly talked about their feelings with me. Cathy's memories were vivid and seemed very real, as did her feelings. She and her dad cried in each other's arms at one point and it was a cathartic moment for both of them. It was as if David was saying he was sorry for his dad's behavior and his own ignorance. Cathy also felt she needed to apologize for telling David and giving him information in the latter years of his life that would negatively impact him and render his helpless in a way. Cathy also realized, with the help of family work, that the kind of closure she wasn't conscious of needing was for her father to protect her, even if only symbolically, now that her grandfather was gone.

David spent many therapy sessions exploring his feelings of regret that he hadn't been there to shield Cathy from being abused by his father. He spent equally as many sessions forgiving his father and forgiving himself.

Jane Isay in her book "Walking on Eggshells" said, "Many young people told me how much they resent being given advice by their parents and how the narrowing of eyes in judgment makes them run for cover. As adults they have the power to distance themselves from their parents, and they use that power when they need to."

One of our adult male patients, coming into a session to consult about his aging mother, explained it this way: "If I am driving on a road and a friend pulls up next to me and asks me where I am going, I tell him I am on my way to a friend's house, but if my mom pulls up next to me on that very same road and asks me where I am headed, I reply in somewhat an abrupt manner, "Why do you need to know?"

As in this above example, the adult child's parent inquiry is seen as intrusive whereas the same question from a peer is welcomed and answered without stirring any negative feeling.

One of the tools we are referring to here is the CBT (Cognitive Behavioral Technique) of 'reframing'. With this learned approach a patient can be taught to phrase problems, situations or concerns in a new light, one that symbolizes strengths and points out the positive rather than concentrating on the negative, Some of the elderly patients we counseled learned to view their dependency upon their adult child (or children) as an opportunity for closeness and bonding, rather than a reason for feeling inadequate or powerless.

Another one of our patients said that she has a hard time communicating with her mother. Whenever her mother babysat, she would do the wash, the dishes, vacuum or wash the kitchen and bathroom floors. Our patient described how she felt: "When mom cleans my house, I feel as if she is negatively judging my housekeeping abilities. It's as if she thinks that if she doesn't do the job, it won't get done. I resent her implication, and I wish she would stop. I've told her on several occasions that her cleaning my house annoys me, but she pooh-poohs my feelings and does what she wants." Clearly, the only problem with communication is the assumption that it has been achieved. When our patient presented this as an issue seriously impacting on her relationship with her mother, we scheduled a joint session and invited her mother to attend. Her mother was happy to be included and the session went remarkably well. A meeting of the minds as well as the bodies occurred. The mother said knowing that her daughter had three little children and a limited income it was her extreme joy to feel helpful when she visits. When her daughter shared how she felt judged as "an incompetent housewife" when her mother cleans, her mother said, "Just the opposite! I don't know how you do what you do. You are an incredible wife, mother and house wife, I never dreamed you felt that way." The rest of the session was spent trying to work within the comfort level of my patient in accepting a limited amount of 'non-judgmental' assistance from her mom, without conflicting feelings.

Our clinical experience has taught us that, although it is usually the senior parent who needs help from the adult child, sometimes the adult child (in middle years) needs the support of the senior parents, both emotionally and even physically.

Maria was 52 when she came to therapy and she may not have started treatment if not for her rehabilitation center suggesting she continue to talk to a professional after she left their facility. Maria had experienced a series of strokes that left her disabled in a variety of ways. She needed a walker to ambulate and she had lost a lot of sensation on one side of her face, in addition to some speech loss.

Although the neurologist and physical therapist told Maria that, in time, it would be likely that she would regain a lot of her strength and the numbness she felt in her face would dissipate, Maria was skeptical and spent many sessions talking about her fears and worries moving forward in her life, particularly since she did not envision herself with a partner. Maria also told us that she never had faith in the prospect of remarrying or even dating since her divorce two years earlier. The anticipation of living alone at this time left her feeling very sad and anxious. This coupled with the notion that she would also need physical help, even if just temporarily, gave our patient a negative outlook in general. It was no wonder that Maria would react to her mother's suggestion to help her with daily chores and personal care with much hesitation, which later evolved into guilt feelings and eventually depression. After all, her mother Rachel had been widowed for 5 years and she was a youthful 77-year-old woman who had her own, very independent lifestyle of traveling with friends and pursuing hobbies.

Rachel lived alone and was content with that arrangement. However, when she joined her daughter for a family session, she explained that it was not a hardship for her, financially or otherwise, to leave her apartment for a time and move in with Maria to help her until she too was independent again. In Rachel's own words: "Helping my daughter would afford me a whole new purpose in life. Yes, I am keeping busy but this is an opportunity to be there for someone whom I dearly love and in such an important way. My life had lost this kind of meaning for quite some time. Maria needs me now: I haven't felt needed in years." These words left Maria almost shocked. She had never thought her mother needed more purpose and only imagined herself a burden should Rachel decide to become her caretaker. Opening up a dialogue in therapy proved to be beneficial to both mother and daughter. Maria was able to express her concerns about Rachel possibly being "cheated out of a more satisfying social life," and Rachel needed help phrasing her concern without sounding as though she was infantilizing her middle-aged daughter. Maria was told that her mother could join a session again at any time should they need mediation along the way, especially if the period of time she needed her mother exceeded either of their expectations.

Getting the message that adult children need a different kind of parenting is not an easy thing to digest, and working on developing new tools of communication for parents and adult children can be quite challenging, and also most rewarding. There are many instances in therapy, we can both recount, in which it seems like a cloud of conflict and confusion lifts to reveal a clear path to a shift in adult parenting. At those times, our patients gain insight along with a sense of mastery over new parenting ground. Often, the adult son or daughter and the senior parent already possessed the knowledge about the kind of changes they needed to consider and once executed, they rejoiced in the positive effects it produced in their family interactions.

8. Torn Hearts Can be Mended

Morris (1996) discusses the prevalence of depression among the elderly and states there is a high percentage of depression in the elderly and an even higher amount that goes untreated. We have seen many senior patients in therapy for depression and, in our experience, they have responded well to a variety of interventions, from cognitive behavioral techniques and poetry to psychodynamic psychotherapy and role playing. In some instances, a psychiatric consult for medication becomes necessary and in other cases, seniors are instead opting to be medicated by their internist on low doses of anti-depressants and/or anti-anxiety medications. We strongly endorse seeing a psychiatrist and recommend the senior patient talk it over with their primary physician, someone who has treated them for many years and whom they trust and respect.

In those cases, in which patients enter into counseling due to grief, a great deal of support and understanding becomes one of the main ingredients of treatment. The clinical supervision, work experience and time Barbara has invested in doing bereavement counseling has taught her that losses have their own individual and unique meaning each time they occur and grief has its own timeline. Many patients come into therapy for the primary purpose of finding an objective, caring individual who will not rush them through their grief or dictate when it is time to resume activities or start new involvements. Many senior patients have expressed an added sadness and frustration when their family members and friends stop talking about the deceased family member in their presence. Instead they would like someone to make a reference to their loved one and they would also appreciate feeling it is OK if they initiate talking about memories they hold dear. One female patient, Beverly, said, "It is hard enough that my friends are uncomfortable asking me about my health now that it is deteriorating, but it is much more difficult to absorb the loss of my husband when it feels taboo to bring up his name in their company." Another patient related to Barbara that while he received a lot of benefit from attending an eight-week bereavement group, he was surprised that the only group offered to him after that entailed a membership of older adults who were ready to 'move on with their lives' and plan social events and trips together. This male patient explained that what he needed was a continuation of grief counseling with others who also lost spouses rather than a social group that needed to form new friendships and partnerships with the opposite sex. According to Knight (1996), the older person is expected by family and friends to have anticipated the loss and there is a misperception that the older individual has little or nothing to look forward to, therefore they need not be encouraged to express emotion or talk about the future.

One of our patients, Ruth, shared that she felt her friends wanted her to forget her husband after he died since "they stopped talking about him after the second year and changed the subject if I brought him up in conversation." Seniors can feel even more slighted or hurt when their own families cease to mention the name of the deceased spouse and sometimes there is guilt felt associated with talking about a deceased husband or wife in the presence of an adult child who is also grieving. A patient named Alan once said: "My mom and I did not mention my dad after the first year following his death and I think it was because each of us projected that the other couldn't handle it, when in fact I would have felt comforted sharing memories about him. Who knows: maybe she would have too."

Sometimes, in subsequent years after a loss, when the waters feel calm, a surviving spouse starts again to feel the waves of grief hitting shore. It may be a strong association brought about by an event, an important anniversary, a memory that is triggered by seeing someone from the past, and it may also be independent of any particular precipitant. It is just there or, in the words of a female patient in therapy two years after bereavement counseling, "It sneaks up on you and pats you on the back like an old friend." This patient taught us that old friends are not always easy to entertain. The pain of loss after time has passed can be very hard to absorb and it can feel almost like the original loss or even more severe. It is for this reason (among others) that Barbara refers to the book "Mending the Torn Fabric: A Book for Those Who Grieve and Those Who Want to Help Them", by Sarah Brabant. The book is, in fact, what she calls her "grief bible" as it describes in the most poignant terms the process of grieving by utilizing a metaphor of fabric, with its weave and mended tears.

Brabant (1996) uses the metaphor of a piece of fabric being the material of one's life, and mourning for a loved one becomes a process of knowing how big the tear in one's fabric is and then deciding how one will mend it. Barbara has found it useful to suggest that certain patients, usually those who benefit from visualizations, affirmations, and the catharsis writing can have, acquire a copy of Brabant's book and then a separate blank notebook or journal to record feelings and thoughts while in therapy for grief. Some patients will take the metaphor further by adding their own descriptions of their torn fabric, with its many different weaves, tears and techniques for repairing the tears. One patient used the metaphor of "fusing fabric" onto her already existing fabric, as a way of describing support received in psychotherapy. Another patient expressed her feelings about having another partner after her husband died, stating: "There are no replacement threads in my damaged fabric. The only fabric that feels and looks right to me is the one my husband and I created the day we committed to one another."

These and other analogies can be powerful and can aid in the therapeutic treatment. They provide a vehicle for discussing a very painful topic such as loss and they paint a visual picture for the patient and family members to look at all at once or with gradual glimpses.

Nancy was 72 years old when her son died suddenly, at age 48. Her son had not been ill and, according to his surviving mom, prided himself in living a healthy lifestyle in terms of exercise, nutrition and avoidance of stress wherever possible. Three months after Robert died, Nancy's husband died as well. Nancy was convinced that her spouse had "died of a broken heart" since he too was physically in excellent health most of his adult life and this was also so sudden.

Nancy came for grief counseling and called it a "double hit", meaning she had just begun to grieve the loss of her son, when she was "bombarded by another major loss, my husband Jacob." Although Jacob had made statements about not being able to survive his son's death, Nancy believed that Jacob would be by her side for many years to come. She thought that together they would find the needed resolve to continue living their lives with quality and purpose and, at the same time, keep the memory of Robert alive and deeply cherished.

Counseling with Nancy was a very different experience than it had been with others suffering losses. While she talked about needing support and finding ways to gain the strength to face life without her family, she continued to help others in the extended family and in her volunteer work for Cancer Care. In her younger years, Nancy had been a freelance writer and so reading and writing had been a big part of her life. Therefore Brabant's book and other self-help books and journal writing came naturally to her. It was a method of communication she often chose above any other to express her feelings. Nancy found it particularly helpful to write a journal entry after reading a meaningful portion of one of her books and would mail the entry to me so we could talk about it in the next session. She related to me, following several months of this treatment technique, that it was one of the most powerful ways for her to emotional relief from the overwhelming losses in her life.

Samuel, a strikingly handsome man in his mid-eighties, was devastated by the death of his wife and soulmate, Rebecca. Married sixty-two years, his wife was hospitalized for a minor surgical procedure and died suddenly, two days later from an infection she contracted in the hospital. Inconsolable, Samuel could not wrap his head around the fact that she died so needlessly and so quickly. They had so much "life" planned and she was ripped away from him so unexpectedly, so abruptly! He had no time to tell her all the things he intended to tell her "someday". After the funeral the house was filled with family and friends coming and going at all hours of the day and night. They tried to help him bridge the enormous gap that he felt represented his life before and after Rebecca's death.

When, in time, people stopped calling and visiting, he found himself in a deep depression. After several months his children urged him to join a bereavement group to help him mourn her passing. He resisted with everything in his being, saying, "I don't need to listen to anyone talk about their loss, I don't care about them, and I don't want them to know what I am going through, it's private and I want to keep it that way."

As more time passed his children noticed that this giant of a man, who was so dynamic and vital before Rebecca's death, had become increasingly despondent and immobile. They were afraid that he wasn't taking his medication or eating properly. They finally had a family intervention and his children proclaimed that he needed to see a therapist. "We explained to him that we were grieving our mother's death too, and not only had we lost our mother, but we were watching our father slip away from us as well." They convinced him, amid fierce protestations, that he begin a treatment program with me for a trial period of a month. If he felt that this was not working, he could stop and they would consider other options. Reluctantly, he agreed, and our work began.

Samuel spent several minutes of our first session together unable to speak coherently and crying uncontrollably. As I watched and waited for him, I saw a man who appeared defeated and destroyed. He seemed a shell of what his children told me was his former self. When he was able to finally speak, I asked if he could tell me what was going through his mind. He thought for a moment and said, "I feel as if half of me was buried with my wife and I long to join her in the grave. She was such a good woman; it's not fair for her to be gone and me to remain. Why? Why did this have to happen? Why her and not me?"

Our ensuing sessions were spent recalling every aspect of Samuel's life with his beloved wife and all the wonderful meanings their relationship had for Samuel. He began with their very first meeting and I noticed how he was animated and eager to recall every detail of the event. Over time he continued to reflect about the milestones of their lives together, and I noticed that his crying was much less intense, and less frequent. One day in treatment he said, "Every corner of every room in our little house is filled with her memory." We discussed how important it was for him to acknowledge her continuing presence in his life. Samuel was able to tell me that the consistent and attentive listening he got from the therapeutic relationship contributed in great part to his healing. He said it was excruciating for friends who knew them well to hear him speak of the loss of his wife and the deep emptiness that remained for him daily, therefore individual therapy had become an irreplaceable component of his existence at that time. This clinical experience and many others had taught us that one of the most essential things a clinician can do for a grieving patient is to listen. True empathy can only occur in those instances in which the therapist does not take the person away from his or her pain, but rather stays in the moment, regardless of how sad or hard it may be.

Several months of treatment 'under his belt', Samuel asked if it was OK for him to invite his children to participate in his treatment. He felt it was important for him to share his thoughts and feelings with them in the safe, nurturing environment my office had become for him. When our conjoint sessions began, I set the framework for our work together by beginning a discussion that acknowledged Samuel's history of hard work and long hours. I also praised him for his willingness to openly share feelings with his family that were not easy to disclose. As a precursor to our first session I told the family members that each person would have a chance to speak, but there would be no interruptions when someone is talking. They all agreed to the ground rules.

At the outset, Samuel was able to thank his children for loving and caring so much for him that they 'forced' him into treatment, but ultimately he was the one who decided to 'do the work'. Several conjoint sessions later, there was free and easy communication between the family members, as each person recalled memories of Rebecca in a loving, poignant way. Samuel said that he now realizes, through our therapy work, that he does not have to 'get on with his life' and put the past behind him. He knows that he is free to go on with his life without cutting out a large piece of his past, his memories of Rebecca. They all know that there will be times when his tears will flow, and sadness will accompany them, but these moments will not consume his life, they will be a natural part of his life, for as long as it takes.

The process of therapy, with Jim and Nora, was a series of numerous small steps. Each found it extremely difficult, initially, to talk about the loss of their son yet each wanted to, as a way of keeping the memory of him alive. Jim, and especially Nora, found photos the most helpful way to begin to bridge the gap between the pain of loss and the need to stay connected to the person they loved most. We spent parts of many sessions looking at photographs and the couple shared stories about Michael in his younger years. It seemed to be an enormous comfort for Nora and some to Jim as well. On a few occasions, Nora brought another few photos that she came across when cleaning Michael's old bedroom and she related that she felt warmed by Jim's reaction. Jim told us that he was experiencing pleasure in relation to making his wife come alive in that session; therefore we surmised it had a therapeutic value for each of them, in their own unique way. Although Jim was reactive to the photos and stories Nora brought to the session, he also needed another vehicle to help him express the feelings that he had buried for some time. Jim took the suggestion to write a letter to his son and he chose to start the letter with the statement "Michael, there are things I wanted to say to you but never had the chance..." The letter continued for at least another two pages. Jim came to realize that, in addition to mourning the painful loss of his son, he was blaming himself for outliving him and although he recognized it may have been an irrational thought, it was what he felt and that needed to be acknowledged. The therapy sessions, and, in particular, the letter writing technique provided Jim with some ways to begin working through some of the grief and as he did, Nora received benefit as well. She felt closer to her husband as a result of sharing deeply felt emotions they had in common. They found a way to communicate they never knew they needed before counseling.

Probably one of the most difficult cases in my practice involved an older couple who came to therapy after losing their 46-year-old son Bradley. As Joe, the 76-year-old husband said: "There is nothing more painful and unnatural than living longer than one's child and I can't imagine ever recovering from it." Joe and his wife Miriam told me they were experiencing some marital problems prior to their son getting diagnosed with cancer but they rallied around Bradley and made giving support the central theme of their lives until the day they lost him. Their support came in the form of money and emotional stability and as Miriam put it, "It was often easier to give monetary support as the pain I felt daily made it hard to appear strong in the presence of Bradley."

Both Joe and Miriam agreed that their problems paled in comparison to what their son was enduring. They witnessed what they described as the pending loss of his life as a husband and father, combined with the dread of waking up each day in physical pain trying to figure out how to gain some needed strength to handle it all. In some respect, Bradley's illness seemed to have brought the couple closer together as though they knew that he could draw strength from them in acting as a unit and it sometimes made the couple a stronger team as a result. When Bradley died, that resolve went with him, and they each isolated in their grief and turned inward. The silence grew between them until the pain became unbearable. It was then that they decided to give their marriage a "shot", as Jim said, to see if they could repair the damage done. They called and made an appointment for counseling soon after.

As a mental health therapist, it was difficult to assess which of their two problems was causing the most discomfort and pain. The tragic death of their son and the shaky condition of their marriage before his illness were both fertile grounds in which to begin work. We decided to start from the beginning and chronicle some of the events in their marital history. It was a bit unusual to find a couple from different backgrounds who each remembered a very stable, secure upbringing within their families of origin, yet that's what Jim and Miriam each recalled. They had each witnessed their own parents survive many different kinds of struggles and they claimed it made their families more cohesive. My patients realized that despite their problems they never sought therapy before their son's death as they had consistently learned to work out their differences the way their parents had years ago. When their son Bradley got diagnosed with a fatal kind of cancer, every value and ideal drastically changed, got challenged or was thrown out the window.

In therapy Joe and Miriam realized that they had used their parents' staunch example of keeping their problems secret and not 'airing their dirty linen' for others to see. Their parents stoically resolved their differences and no one was the wiser about who suffered or how their life may have been diminished in the process. Jim added that in those days only 'crazy' people sought treatment from a therapist or a psychiatrist.

Mourning the loss of their son sadly brought this couple to their knees, both literally and figuratively. On the one hand their loss found them returning to their church for spiritual solace and comfort and to restore their faith. On the other hand, they had each hit their lowest point emotionally when they buried their son. In a last ditch effort to salvage whatever was left to save of their marriage, they resorted to therapy. Both of these were positive, life-affirming steps to becoming whole again after an unspeakable tragedy. Joe and Miriam continued with their couple therapy to learn a better, kinder, more loving way to handle conflicts and how to express their emotions in a non-judgmental, constructive, caring format.

In the book, "Through Thick and Thin", the authors compliment and encourage couples to enter therapy at any stage of their marriage to resolve conflicts and help with communication problems. It is never too late to want to work at bettering a stale relationship. In seeking therapy couples can expect to have help in promoting healthy lifestyle practices, assistance in adapting to losses subsequent to chronic illnesses or fatal accidents, and suggestions or referrals to community resources such as religious institutions or self-help groups that will enhance a sense of belonging and affiliation. They can also expect to diminish their anxieties and fears related to the aging and retirement process.

When a loved one dies it is natural to experience a wrenching and perhaps a sense of 'survival guilt' in the grieving process. Many people think that if "they only" had done more, they could have (if not prevented the death altogether) at least delayed it a bit. Since it is not 'natural' in the order of life for a parent to outlive their child, no matter how old the child is at the time of death, a parent may have tried to bargain with G-d, asking Him to spare their child and take them instead. When the child dies and they find themselves still alive, their anger at G-d escalates and their expression of grief becomes more profound. The time immediately following the funeral is generally a time when family and friends try to show their love and support to the bereft individual. However, many people do not know how to properly express their sympathy. Empty 'well-meaning' phrases such as, *"she's gone to a better place"*, or *"he is not suffering anymore"*, or *"she wouldn't want you to be crying this way"*, or *"he lived a rich, full life"*, or *"the loss grows dimmer with time"*, and many, many more such as these, although empathetic, do not do much for the survivor. What they need are people to encourage them to talk about their feelings and allow them to mourn their loss. The suggestion for them to join a bereavement group or see a therapist (when they are ready) can be a very thoughtful, meaningful and helpful expression of your concern. For a friend who is mourning the need to be heard and listened to by a professional in the field can be an invaluable gift.

9. How Therapy Helps

We have experienced times in which our colleagues seemed surprised when we told them the age of our oldest patient in psychotherapy, yet we didn't feel it was unusual to have an 85-year-old patient in treatment. It was rather a function of putting out feelers that we like working with seniors, and we also value what we learn from them as well as delight in the changes they are amenable to making.

Therapy serves different purposes for different individuals. Some people enter into a commitment to attend sessions only on a short term basis (i.e. 3-6 months) because they want to focus on a specific problem or set of related problems. Others require long-term treatment to maintain a kind of equilibrium in their relationships and in their own moods, and to break the isolation of living alone and/or feeling lonely. There are those senior patients who come in for bereavement counseling and decide somewhere along the road, whether it is verbalized or not, that they also want to work on other issues they hadn't initially intended to explore. As clinicians, we know that the presenting problem may be far from what is really ailing the patient or it may segue into other areas that had not yet been revealed as having importance to the person.

In our work with seniors and the elderly, we find that a great deal of support and guided listening is needed in order to help the patient navigate the often rough waters of aging and all it brings with it (i.e. physical illness, limitations, loss of loved ones, loss of independence and intergenerational communication problems). Many of the elderly patients we see strongly feel their voice has been hushed either by physicians or other health care professionals and sadly even by family members. One of our patients (age 83) told us that her internist stopped making eye contact with her once her son Richard began to accompany her to the medical appointments. She commented, in one of our sessions, that physicians need to understand that the lack of eye contact, so common in situations when elderly patients are accompanied by a family member, "makes us feel invisible". With a little assertiveness training, this patient learned to be her own advocate and only ask for her son to be in the room as needed to consult with the doctor. This change gave the patient a boost to her self-esteem and, as a result, she felt less helpless.

A cognitive behavioral approach seems appropriate much of the time in therapy (particularly short-term therapy) and we have found it to be effective in helping the senior and elderly patient start to challenge some faulty, negative thinking, the kind that usually triggers depression. According to Knight (1996), behavioral therapy is valued as a chosen method of treatment with elderly patients because it "is committed to a spirit of optimism about the possibility for change in older people," (p.20). Additionally, the author states that controlled research studies have confirmed that therapy in later life is quite effective for treating depression. Mediation between the older patient and their family member is additionally quite useful and can break down barriers to open communication that may have existed for years. In some more unfortunate situations, estrangement in families persists and takes a toll on a parent and also on an adult child. The more we conduct psychotherapy with senior patients, the more we come to realize how important a supportive family network can be. This is one of the reasons that family work can be essential to add to a patient's treatment plan. Not all seniors are amenable to family therapy and will instead opt to discuss their family dynamics in individual treatment. In some instances, they have a family member come in one time to meet the treating professional. Some of those initial sessions naturally develop into family treatment or at least a few more sessions to work on resolving an issue. In still other instances they remain for just one session for consultation. Even in those instances in which the family member attended only one session, we usually witnessed some degree of movement in the family dynamics, if not outright change. It may have happened because the senior patient felt supported for the first time, or the adult daughter or son for the first time understood a struggle their parent was experiencing. Either way, having a third party present to mediate facilitates many different kinds of positive changes in behavior.

One could be tempted to ask if there are any specific limitations or challenges for the senior when entering into therapy. Colleagues have even confided in each of us that they do not particularly enjoy working with this age group when doing treatment. We have been discouraged to hear that many people, professionals and lay people alike, believe that once people reach a certain age, they are not inclined to change, listen to guidance from others or make new and different choices. This has not been our history treating the senior population. Instead, we have repeatedly encountered male and female patients in their 60's, 70's and 80's who are eager to change, communicate better and grow emotionally and spiritually, both internally and within their families. This is not to say that there do not exist some unique challenges for the senior or elderly patient. Knight (2000) speaks about a number of factors responsible for physiological and psychological changes within the older patient and they can impact therapy. These include such factors as: 1) a slowing down of cognitive processes; 2) a decline in one's ability to reason; and 3) memory loss. We not only validate the above factors, but we also agree with Knight, in that therapists working with an older population need to adapt to the developmental and physiological changes while supporting their patients with an understanding, open mindset about differences that surface with age.

In those cases in which the adult child is living with the aging parent or vice versa, coming in to a therapy session can prove to be fruitful, since it provides the treating clinician with another view of the senior patient. The adult son or daughter may reveal some of the significant changes in their parent's functioning and this oftentimes opens up a dialogue for exploring what the aging parent may need emotionally or physically. Being able to assist a healthy discussion between a parent and adult child can sometimes be the impetus for healthier relationships between family members in very substantial ways too.

When Herman first called me to make an appointment, he was so distraught that I had a hard time making sense of his story. He was a man in his seventies, trained originally to become a concert pianist, but had abandoned his artistic ambitions for a small business in order to raise a family. Once his business started to fail, when he was in his mid-sixties, he fell into a depression. The depression, untreated, became an incapacitating one, requiring hospitalization more than once. Although his mood improved after he was hospitalized, Herman described a feeling of "being battered by the blues" as each time he went through another bout of depression. He again felt he had suffered a great deal and was left with the scars to prove it. I asked him how long he was thinking of seeing a therapist before he sought my help, and he replied: "This time, I only waited weeks, not months or years."

During the first year of outpatient therapy, I saw Herman through two bouts of depression, in which his daily functioning was compromised somewhat. He had become inconsistent with attending to his appearance and he had stopped driving and was relying on his youngest son Bernard to take him to doctor's visits. Both Herman and Bernard were in agreement that he was too distracted to drive and continuing would only put him, and possibly others, at risk. During these two years of therapy, Herman was amenable to antidepressant medication, something that repelled him in the past. He eventually emerged from depression without requiring hospitalization and was able to return to his baseline functioning. I came to learn that Herman's baseline functioning included a clinging dependency. For example, he called me several times between sessions and he was highly manipulative, giving me all sorts of reasons to change his session day and time. It didn't surprise me that Herman's previous therapist related that he did not like treating him due to his irritating, manipulative ways.

I soon realized his pattern: Herman was not going to keep appointments on rainy days, or hours before noon, and he would surely cancel if something better came along. I knew we would need to put in place some kind of structure with limits; otherwise I would soon be experiencing only negative counter-transference like his previous therapist. My patient agreed to a plan: he would only call to reschedule if there was an emergency and he would adhere to the policy of 24 hours notice. Herman even agreed to try and make it into the office when the weather was nothing more than a light drizzle.

I was told during the first few weeks of treatment that my patient had been raised in a household in which he was the only male child and he regularly manipulated his two sisters into doing his chores for him. When Herman married, he chose a partner whom he was convinced would wait on him hand and foot and he was right in his perception. If he had been working late and then went to bed, he called to his wife to turn out the lights, despite the fact that she was often asleep by that time.

During the first several sessions, it was revealed to me that Herman had an intense yearning for love and approval from his father, which was in conflict with his intense competitiveness with him. He acted as if he couldn't become a successful adult unless he was able to beat or outsmart his dad in business. That seemed to be the reason that he persisted against odds and without capital in the same business as his father. His erratic actions toward his father alternated between the pursuits of these two alternatives. Herman had always trusted his father more than his neurotic mother. He even tried working for him once when he had given up his career in music. He wished to prove to his father that he could also be a good businessman. He felt that this was the only way he could finally earn his father's respect.

The interactions with his son Bernard closely resembled the relationship he had with his own father. In other words, Bernard worked hard for his father's approval and when it wasn't forthcoming, he became sad and angry. In fact, Herman described Bernard's mood as "despondent" during some of those times. Herman blamed himself for his son's reaction as he explained that, in his eyes, he must have perpetuated an unhealthy cycle that began with his father many years before.

I knew there was a lot of family work that needed addressing. It became apparent not only from the patient's recounting of family history and current climate of the family relationships, but additionally I sensed it in the transference he made to me. So often Herman misread cues and heard negative undertones that I strongly believed he imagined were based in the truth. It was as though I was observing the unfolding of a father-son relationship laden with friction, one that Herman had with his dad, and then re-enacted with his son and now with me. I tried to encourage a family consultation with Herman and Bernard but Herman was not amenable to the idea. He told me that he was not willing to risk his son becoming angry and, in Herman's own words, "Bernard does not value therapy and sees it as an invasion of his privacy." Instead, I tried to assist Herman in improving his interactions with his son and helped him make those links between the family dynamics of father and son, dynamics that had a generational kind of repetition.

Prior to discussions in therapy, Herman described family dinners that traditionally arose whenever someone's birthday was approaching. According to my patient's descriptions, the family seemed tense around him and Bernard. Herman referred to the tension as their sensing unfinished business between the two. There was so much they both chose not to say it seemed as if old conflicts from Bernard's childhood were also rooted in

Herman's relationship with his dad. Herman did not experience good role modeling from his father. I tried to provide the healthy kind of parenting and mentoring that was so lacking. There were times it backfired. There were moments in which Herman rejected the parent role model or a substitute parental love, making it appear as though he didn't need or want it, when in fact I sensed that he was craving it. He would distance himself from me emotionally. He would psychologically shut down in our sessions, which often came as a reaction to my attempts to reach out to him to provide some basic caring and acceptance.

In one of our sessions I quoted from a poem I had once read. The quote was: "A long conviction of worthlessness builds strong walls. The nearer you approach me the blinder I strike back. I fight the very thing I cry out for."

I asked Herman if the quote held any significance for him. He thought for a long, long time and finally whispered, "Those words resonate inside of me. They remind me of how I treat my son Bernard. The thing I want most from him is his love and acceptance, and when he appears to be kind and loving to me I push him away and castigate him. Why? Why do I do this?" We spoke for quite some time about his relationship with Bernard, and then I asked him if his relationship with his own father was similar. Although I had broached this topic many times before in our sessions together, this time he seemed to understand that he himself continued to re-enact the father-son scenario, that had been so destructive to him as a child, with his son Bernard. The lines from the poem connected in some visceral way that we had never been able to achieve before. Once the realization took hold, and Herman internalized the enormity of it, our therapy sessions took on a positive spin. He seems to sincerely want to correct the mistakes he made in parenting his son, and is well on the way towards meeting his goal.

Following is a story which exemplifies the benefits of therapy for a troubled, elderly mother. Mirabel agreed, after three months of therapy, to have a joint session with her son Andy. The patient's middle-aged son divorced his second wife and was going through his own set of problems. He expressed concern that his mother was in need of support from him and also from a mental health professional. When Andy came into the session his first statement was about viewing himself as "someone who would not normally come to see a shrink". He later explained that his first wife was a social worker and he always resented the way she analyzed him and pushed him to talk about his feelings. Now, however, he was agreeing to come in to see his mother's therapist only because he was concerned for her.

What surfaced in that one session was that both Mirabel and Andy suffered from depression, and each was hesitant to bring it up to the other. It made perfect sense that each could quickly recognize depression in the other more easily than they could in themselves. The session provided us with more history and even more importantly, some personal observations, particularly Andy's. For example, he realized that his mother needed more contact with him and he became more willing to fulfill that need. He also realized that he avoided his mother because seeing her was a painful reminder that she is aging and he will one day lose her. Mirabel, on the other hand, didn't want to make demands as she felt that Andy was deeply sad about his failed marriages and reluctant to see his mother for fear of being criticized.

It isn't as though one therapy session could be held responsible for identifying all of the above, but rather that it gave the patient and her son a forum for expressing feelings, openly and without judgment. It also left the door open so that, should the need arise again, either of them could ask for a family session. As Andy left the appointment he said, that "Shrinks are not all that bad," while Mirabel sat on the couch looking surprised, yet pleased.

Another example of how therapy can help is found in the following case history of a man and his son. Leon, a retired lawyer in his early eighties came to see me stating he was having difficulty sleeping and was "fed up and frustrated" with the conversations with his adult son Arthur. In fact, according to the identified patient, their conversations often "don't feel like conversations at all". Instead they felt like the aftermath of war; a cold war. Leon described a consistent presence of tension and subsequent uncomfortable silences that lasted as long as weeks, sometimes even months. Leon was holding back tears in one of our sessions, as he expressed feeling such emptiness around family holidays, when Arthur "wouldn't show up." He would tell his three sisters that he would be attending and, at the very last moment, he would call to cancel or not call at all. I asked Leon if he or his other adult children confronted Arthur about his unexpected lack of attendance and the patient explained that fear was holding him back from confronting his son, a fear that could possibly be realized if the family ties were completely severed by Arthur. I also asked Leon how he and his son reconnected following one of their 'cold wars' and he told me that he did all the outreach to Arthur, otherwise "there would have been no contact." Their conversations sometimes ended in stormy arguments in which one of them would hang up abruptly and Leon would call Arthur back and leave a message on his answering machine, since Arthur wouldn't pick the phone up at those moments. Leon described the distancing as something nonverbal, rather than words expressed by Arthur. Leon told me he would notice that Arthur became non-communicative and wouldn't even look in his direction on those rare times that they did see one another.

One of Leon's goals for therapy was to learn how to approach his son in a way that would be productive for their relationship and lead to improved communication rather than the faulty kind they had. He wanted to 'break the pattern', and end the cycle of pain created by both of them repeatedly.

Leon said, in one of our early sessions, that "everything each of us says seems to fall on deaf ears." The patient described a conversation in which each would become defensive and criticize the other, rather than hear the stated position of the other person. In Leon's words, Arthur felt he was only sympathetic and understanding toward others in their family circle, but never to him. According to Leon, "Arthur acted like when I asked him what his plans were for the weekend, if he didn't have any, he thought that I was negatively judging him for not organizing his schedule or planning things sensibly in advance." The very same thing would happen when they met face to face and it was nonverbal at those times. Arthur would sense a kind of disapproval in his father's face or body language that just wasn't there. Instead, the patient elaborated, "I was confused by the strained answers I would get from Arthur or the impatience in his voice when it was merely a simple question I was asking." Leon expressed feeling aware of this vicious cycle yet he got caught up in it while talking to his son. He recalled an incident in which he called Arthur and asked him innocently what he was doing at home. Arthur immediately became "snappy" according to Leon and raised his voice, stating, "You are accusing me of not working when I was only going in an hour late today due to a personal errand I took care of." Leon said he wasn't even thinking that and knew his son's perception was not true but he still got swept up in an argument that lasted 15 minutes, leaving each of them bruised, like "wounded soldiers after battle." The patient didn't remember who hung up first or if it was simultaneous. At the next family function, one of the rare times that Arthur attended, they hardly spoke at all. Our sessions taught Leon to do less of the asking of questions and more of the listening to his son, making an attempt to truly hear him. Questions, we decided, would be perceived by Arthur the wrong way and sound like an attack. Leon came to understand that the way for this relationship with his eldest child to heal was for him to stay focused when they talked and work at hearing what his son was saying.

Some of the discussions between father and adult son were circular and Leon described a feeling of "chasing my own tail". Some discussions, for example, would involve a simple graph or circular design depicting the chain reaction involved when one has a thought that leads to a feeling and then a subsequent behavior. He said, "I know that when we rehash the past it is futile, yet we return to a discussion about past events and the way each of us handled them poorly, time and time again." Leon further stated that they "talk at each other" and it becomes a contest of who can raise their voice the loudest without blatantly yelling. No one gets heard and no one feels understood, yet no one can stop the cycle.

Therapy was useful in helping Leon get in touch with his own early abandonment issues, as his father left the home when Leon was about six years of age, and Leon rarely saw him after that. Before entering treatment, the patient was convinced that he hadn't felt that loss as being significant since he didn't have his father around for many years of his life anyway. Once these issues were explored over time, Leon realized that he in fact missed his father a great deal and that may explain why he decided to go into the same field (Leon's father was also a lawyer). In this way, Leon could feel close to his father through the professional connection.

During his treatment I learned that Leon was raised by his mother and widowed maternal grandmother. There were no male role models within the family structure and he was doted upon and spoiled by both women. As he matured, he firmly believed that the world was his oyster and was surprised and annoyed when obstacles were thrown in his path. He was so accustomed to having things his own way, that he had a hard time dealing with this reality of life. Later on when he married and the children started coming he was deeply disappointed to discover that his wife's world no longer revolved around him. He enjoyed the 'royal treatment' he received as a child and wanted this to continue into his relationship with his wife and children. He found that idolization in his firstborn son, Arthur. From the earliest time, people described Arthur as "Velcro", since he was so attached to his father. Leon loved the child and adored being put on that pedestal by the bright, handsome, engaging child. As Arthur advanced to manhood, a rivalry steadily grew between them. Leon challenged Arthur and expected more from him than any of his other children. He imposed tremendous pressure when it came to selecting a college, career and ultimately a wife.

The similarities in their personalities were remarkable; both were stubborn, inflexible men. It was no wonder to me as Leon's therapist that there would be conflict in the relationship, given their 'battle' history. Our job, in reaching Leon's objective of learning how to approach his son in a way that would lead to improved communication, was to diffuse the hostility and prepare fertile ground for planting the seeds of harmony between them. For this to happen, I recommended that Leon ask his son to join him in a therapy session.

We rehearsed how Leon was to approach the subject in a soft, gentle manner that would not precipitate another war. We decided to be painfully honest and have Leon 'tell it like it is'. I asked him: "What would you like to say to Arthur?" With tears brimming over the lids of his closed eyes, he whispered, "Arthur, I am eighty four years old. I am an old, sick man. I don't know how many years I have left on this earth, and I am tired of fighting with you each time we speak. I love you and I want to learn how to communicate with you in a kind, tender, nurturing way. I realize that I have been a difficult man, and I want to change, but I need your help. Can we put the hurtful, painful past to rest and move on towards that goal of being the loving father and son we once were? I need you more than you know, and I wish my remaining years could be spent in a loving relationship with you, Arthur, my only son." This was the first time in our treatment together that Leon admitted that he was at least partly to blame for the deficits in their relationship and the first time he admitted he loved and needed his son. This was, in essence, Leon's giant step towards making lasting peace with his son.

The next several steps were even larger. We explained to Leon how a cognitive behavioral approach to treatment could be helpful in improving his relationship with his son. Leon learned first-hand that much of the improvement would be a result of learning to eliminate faulty thinking and substitute healthier ideas that would eventually lead to more appropriate actions. Kraus, Kunik & Stanley (2007) claim that CBT "is effective with older adults," (p.22). The authors explain that short-term therapeutic techniques, such as CBT, focus on problem solving and are a good adjunct, if not substitute, for prescribed psychiatric medications in older adults who might be at a higher risk of adverse side effects than younger patients. Our patient shared that he often thought in terms of catastrophic outcomes when he made plans to see his son. He would tell himself that they were going to either fight or fall into silence, since that's what the past dictated.

In an attempt to aid Leon in increasing his awareness about his distressed thoughts, which stirred up a negative emotion, we suggested Leon keep a self-monitoring log, like the kind suggested by Kraus, et al (2007). Leon would track his symptoms (usually of depression) on paper and write down when they occurred and what was going on at the time. Most importantly, Leon was able to see a connection between physical symptoms, the subsequent thoughts and the behaviors he engaged in during the time his symptoms showed up. This approach was very useful with Leon as he was the kind of person who needed to understand things intellectually and also was a visual learner, therefore paper and pen assignments were most suitable.

After a few months of treatment, Leon decided that he wanted to take it further by asking his son to join him in one of his sessions. We coached Leon to present the invitation to Arthur in a way that would not sound threatening. Leon clearly understood the need for a neutral tone in which he would present an invitation to his son to join a session in order to consult on Leon's behalf and in the hopes of helping the therapist better understand the communication problems Leon was having with him. Here is what he wrote:

> Dear Arthur: I have been in therapy for the past several months and have benefited greatly from the experience. I understand now that I may have been at fault for many of the disagreements we have had. I invite you to attend a therapy session with me to help me learn how to improve my attitude and interaction with you. This is very important to me, and I hope you will accept my invitation to participate so we can bridge the gap between us. Sincerely, Dad.

Joint sessions between an aging parent and an adult child often yield reactions of surprise in one or both family members. The mediation between parent and child can correct false assumptions each have buried or carried around without checking their validity. Likewise, the joint counseling often creates opportunities to work through conflict that couldn't easily be resolved without a third party to hear both sides. To us, one of the best end results of these sessions is the acknowledgement that both parent and child identify with one another's feelings but didn't know that until the treatment began. It can also be refreshing to hear that, to their surprise, the adult child or aging parent may discover in counseling that what the other family member feels or thinks does not depict as negative a scenario as they had imagined.

We have found that as people age their values become narrower and increasingly clear. Most of all, they value their relationships with their children. Their children become their focus in their declining years. They view the relationships with their children as the standard with which they judge their own intrinsic worth. If their children are relatively successful and happy in their own lives, the elderly parent will think that they have done their job well. If they are able to maintain good solid conversations with them, they can rest easy. If, on the other hand, the relationship is strained and rocky, they may internalize the situation as their own 'bad parenting', and suffer from the guilt they claim as their own, or, in the reverse, they blame their children for what is missing in their lives. In either case, the aging parent may be filled with feelings of sadness, resentment, and pain.

Lilly, a woman in her eighties, entered therapy because of the distant relationship she and her husband had with their son, Ralph. The husband and wife were both European immigrants who came to America and subsequently lived through the horror of the Great Depression. The tendency in this type of a household was to live in fear that 'the bottom may soon fall out – again!' These words were spoken by Lilly in one of our sessions and honestly, the fear registered on her face as she talked about it in detail. She told me that parents of her generation worked their fingers to the bone, doing without any luxuries so that their children would get the opportunity of a 'better life'.

Many parents of this generation viewed parenthood as the promise of a second chance to make up for missed opportunities of their own. They saw parenthood as an occasion to offer their child what they themselves were not given by their parents. Most parents did the very best they could with the knowledge and experience they had. Probably they made mistakes along the way, and we're sure many people's 'psyches' have suffered from these mistakes. The terrible thing about being a parent in the forties, fifties and sixties was that were no schools that taught people how to be a good parent. Most parents struggled along using the 'trial and error' method and hoped that in the process they met all the needs of their children, including physical, mental, emotional, spiritual and material needs.

For Lilly and her husband, the better life for her children began with a good education, something they themselves were denied. Lilly's husband disciplined their children, perhaps too rigidly, used corporal punishment too frequently, and often used humiliation, belittling and cursing in order to control the children or get them do their homework. However, this verbal abuse injured and wounded them much deeper than his physical abuse because the child internalized the messages as 'you're no good and never will be', and grew up with damaged (if any) self-esteem.

The parents did everything they could to demand that their children get better grades so that they would be eligible for college. Baseball, roller skating, biking, football, rock and roll were labeled "foolishness", and not accepted. Studies came first, last, and sometimes, always. "My father never played ball with me, or took me to the park or read to me," are often listed in the letter of divorce to parents. Working six days a week at one or two arduous jobs, in order to put food on the table, clothes on the backs and roofs over the heads of their children, were exhausting. Reading to their children, in many cases, was an embarrassment to the parents because they may have been illiterate and would never admit *that* to their child.

"My mother never taught me how to cook, spoke to me about sex, or played house with me," are feminine counterparts of the above. If mother didn't allow you in the kitchen, it was probably because she was doing six things at once and couldn't take the time to explain recipes. If she didn't talk to you about sex, it may have been because she knew next to nothing about sex herself, except that it had something to do with all the children she kept having! Orgasm? She often had no idea what that was from her own personal life; it was just something she may have read about in a romance novel, but never dreamed it could be achieved in her bed.

Enter the eldest child in this family, Ralph (the oldest son), who with much damage to his id, obeys his parents and achieves their ultimate goal for him: a college education! Not only a Bachelor's and Master's degree, but, beyond their wildest dreams, a doctorate! How proud they were of all he had accomplished. Never mind all that they went through, or went without, to allow him the opportunity to go so far. He was their child and they were so proud and happy for him.

When applying for colleges, he purposely chose a college far away from home, several states away. The day he left for college became his literal 'independence day' from the whole brutal family dynamic that he so abhorred. Ralph made a promise to himself that he was never to live in his parent's home again, and it was kept!

Over the years Lilly and her husband felt the uneasiness in their gut at special occasions, such as his high school graduation where Ralph asked them not to wave at him when he walked down the aisle to receive his diploma. There were times when he would not introduce them to his teachers or his friends, times when he ignored them or just asked them not to come to his graduation from graduate school. When he met 'the one girl for him' he coached them on how to act before they were to meet her family. It became increasingly clear that he was ashamed of them. After earning a law degree he married the woman who was the complete opposite of his mother in looks, personality and education. They bought a home far away from his parents and had little to do with them, except for the obligatory holidays or family functions.

On the rare occasions that he was with his parents it was an embarrassment to Ralph that they were working class people who didn't speak the King's English, or use proper grammar. He cringed when he saw how their manners lacked sophistication.

He felt and was, financially, socially and educationally, their superior and was terribly ill at ease in their presence. Being with them reminded him of his impoverished beginnings and the severe beatings he was subjected to as a child by his cruel, callous father. To rectify these feelings of shame and guilt, he just made it his business not to see them unless absolutely necessary.

A successful lawyer, Ralph was the devoted husband and loving father of two. He was active in his community and highly respected in his church. During all those years, Lilly continued to dote on her son from a distance, making excuses to others in the family for his obvious lack of interest in his parents' lives. He rarely sent a card for their anniversary, birthday or other 'Hallmark' holidays. She would wait by the mailbox expectantly, and come back empty-handed and empty-hearted. When she would call him, he would have very little to say and replied in one word answers to her questions.

When Lilly began treatment, we tried to focus on her goals and expectations in order to accomplish something meaningful within a realistic framework. We decided that our goal was not to change her son Ralph, but to accept that he would most likely never live up to her idealized vision of how a son *should be*. What we needed to concentrate on in treatment was what would make her life more meaningful and fulfilled, whether or not Ralph became a participant in it. It appeared to me that Lilly was obsessing over the things she didn't have, such as a meaningful, pleasant relationship with her son Ralph, rather than being grateful for the wonderful things she did have, such as her husband, two married daughters, a married son and twelve grandchildren.

The object of our continuing treatment was to increase the sense of joy in her life and decrease the sorrow. Lilly was anxious to start, but we were soon to find out how much of a payoff it was to her to be the recipient of her friends' pity, to have an ungrateful, thoughtless son. The picture was pure black and white. Lilly was the victim, pure white, and Ralph was the villain, pure black. When Lilly realized the gains that were achieved by perpetuating this perception, she recoiled.

We began weeks of hard work by identifying the feelings and emotions Lilly felt when she complained about Ralph's treatment of her. "When my friends hear how horribly I am treated by my son they rally around me, support me, sympathize with me and constantly affirm that I am a good, kind, loving mother, who doesn't deserve the misery I am served by my son. I feel validated, encouraged and buoyed up by their defense of me. Truth be told, at times I have even exaggerated a story to make him look like more of a demon than he really is, just to gain the sympathy of my friends," Lilly reported. We continued in treatment to recognize and discover what made her value the position of 'victim' in her peers' eyes. "I guess I feel protected and embraced. When my friends hear that I am hurt they nurture me and soothe me and it feels good to be treated with such loving concern and kindness," sighed Lilly.

In the following weeks we spoke about how Lilly could achieve the results she so cherished, without compromising herself by adopting the role of the victim. Our work is ongoing, and filled with discovery and sensitivity. Lilly has been amazed to realize that it is possible for her to change at her age, albeit slowly, taking baby steps to reach her goals. I have observed her demeanor become softer, more confident and self-assured, and less dependent on Richard's opinion of her to feel good about herself. She mentioned that she feels "empowered" in one of our sessions, and less reliant on the opinion of others. "The older I get, maybe the better and wiser I am getting," she remarked.

In ways, children always need their parents, even though they protest too much that they don't. This mutual need was examined by Margaret Hellie Huyck and Susan Frank in a fascinating inter-generational study of adult children and their parents. The most important finding in this study was that *both generations looked to the other for validation* – for the adult children that they were lovable or admirable or acceptable, and for the parents, that they got reasonably good marks in family matters and that, at the end of the day (or a life), their children appreciated them. We, as professionals in the mental health field, have had our own validation, and have found repeatedly, that adult children who traverse these waters while the opportunity still exists have much less unresolved feelings once their parent dies.

Psychoanalyst Jessica Benjamin expands upon this theme of mutual validation in her book, "The Bonds of Love". She makes the strong case that one cannot fully be a whole person without being seen as such by another whole person. "The issue," writes Benjamin, "is not how we become free of the other, but how we actively engage and make ourselves known in relation to the other."

One day, several months later, Lilly reported what seemed to her like a strange phenomenon had occurred, completely unexpected. Ralph, noticing that his parents had not called in quite a while, called them "just to say hello". This phone call was a short but pleasant exchange, with no demands, no hidden agenda, and none of her guilt-instilling subliminal suggestions. It seemed to Lilly that Ralph enjoyed the conversation and she certainly did. He stayed on the phone asking benign questions about his parents' health, plans for their vacation, even a remark about how wonderful Lilly sounded, and he didn't seem in his usual rush to hang up. This phone call was a milestone in the relationship between mother and son. We utilized the positive feelings Lilly had after her son's phone call in our work together. The realization hit her that during that particular phone conversation she had made a conscious effort to change her tone and lighten her mood. She genuinely was thrilled to hear from her son and he sensed that joy in her voice.

Lilly has become more aware of her own negativity, what she terms her "doom and gloom attitude," and other things she does that turn people off, particularly her son. Her work has become clear with regard to her son. She is aware of the fact that things were not back and white, they were mostly grey, and she admits to some of the fault for the holes in their relationship. She knows now that she needs to change her attitude and put some distance between them in order for the wounds to heal. Sometimes it is very hard for Lilly to abandon her old-style ways of thinking, and at times she takes one step forward and two steps back. However, we both look forward to our sessions together and delight in the positive results her therapy has achieved.

Listening to these strong feelings about the aging process is a great privilege and a great responsibility. To deal with these types of intense feelings one cannot issue platitudes such as, "There, there, things will get better dear. Just hang in there." We believe that our role in counseling mature people is to deal in the reality of life, and help our patients see that there is joy to be found in aging. It's just that the losses are more easily seen and identified and the joys may be harder to define. That is what makes our job so challenging. Being able to listen empathetically and compassionately to the pain and suffering in our patients' lives and then become guides to enable and empower our patients to identify the activities and relationships that bring them happiness is an honor that we cherish. In a selfish way, we understand that their voices may very well be our voices in the future, so we are both teachers and students of life at the very same time.

10. Sisters That Share

Most women would agree that they benefit from sharing their feelings with other women within a supportive environment. We have found that senior women especially value group therapy with someone trained to understand the unique issues confronting women 60 years+. Carol's groups for female seniors cover a wide variety of topics including health issues, sexuality, marital/family relationships, aging and the isolation it often brings with it, retirement and grandparenting. When the women leave group sessions, they often exit with the knowledge that they are not alone and a feeling that they are understood by others in similar circumstances. When the group dynamic is processed over the coming week, the patient often begins her sharing the next week with, "Something that was said last week made quite an impression on me and I'd like to address that today."

Some of the patients in Carol's support groups enter into treatment because they are in a crisis, and others enter in the hopes of making connections with peers for a number of reasons. The seniors who participate in a group setting often reach out for support following a series of losses; yet at other times they may feel isolated in their marriages or lonely just because they have been living alone. It is not uncommon for Carol's group members to gain a sense of empowerment as they witness change in others and feel that they may have contributed to the successes of other group participants.

One of the interesting dynamics in a therapeutic group is the reinforcement, respect, encouragement and friendship which develop among the members. Often in group the supporting members point out her strength and power to a woman who has been sharing her insecurity and lack of self-worth. "If you can see yourself through our eyes you would see your value," is a sentiment expressed often in group and puts a life affirming, positive, uplifting spirit into the exchange. When validation such as this is consistently offered to women of low self-esteem, they begin to accept that they are human beings who have intrinsic value and worth and their life has meaning.

Another major factor brought to light in group is the enactment of family dynamics. Often a recurring dynamic is the parent and child or sibling relationship. Despite the fact that Carol is chronologically a peer to many of the women who attend group, she often is seen as the matriarch of the group and is given the authority to be the only parent to the group members who are searching for advice or support. The fact that the women identify with Carol as the parent often means that they see themselves as siblings. With the 10-20 year difference that can be common in group, with women ranging in age from their 60's-80's, it is even easier to perceive others as sisters.

Several women, over time, have stayed in the group for a number of years and as a result, they have been privy to a great deal of personal growth on the part of their group peers. The group, and Carol's role modeling, has assisted the women in learning how to give positive reinforcement to group participants, rather than criticism that doesn't get heard or processed therapeutically.

They have additionally received a good amount of positive reinforcement for the new risks they have taken in their own lives; risks and changes they may have previously minimized or omitted from discussion. Self-esteem noticeably increases when women in groups get validated for their efforts in behaving in new ways. Additionally, the women get a sense of mastery when they try things never before tried and feel especially good when they are reminded to give themselves a little more credit than they used to.

Raised in a culture that didn't give much consideration to women going to college, the women in this group may have graduated from high school, but often did not have the opportunity to go any further with their education. Instead of a traditional college degree they got their MRS Degree when they married. The children started coming and, of course, times had changed drastically since they were in school. In this new era girls were told while they were still in their cribs, that they could be whatever they wanted when they grew up. "Don't settle for being a nurse, be a doctor! Why just be an airline stewardess when you could be a pilot; or a dental assistant when you could be a dentist." The list goes on and on. So the young women went to law school, medical school, earned doctorates in education and became hospital administration, etc. By the time their proud mothers become grandmothers and have wandered into the group, they sometimes experience a lack of self-esteem due to what they feel is their lack of a formal education.

One woman in particular from the group comes to mind. Her name is Patti and she suffers from an inferiority complex because she never had the opportunity to attend college. She is an extremely bright woman with wonderful insight and is regarded by all her friends as a caring, empathetic, outgoing, knowledgeable woman. However, she constantly denigrated herself as foolish and stupid, although anyone who knows her knows that this is untrue. She even compares herself negatively with her own daughter, who is a surgeon, and of course she feels as if she comes up short. She gets upset when her daughter doesn't treat her with respect and contributes it to the fact that they are on different educational levels. She thinks her daughter talks "down" to her and is condescending and that reinforces her low sense of self-worth and lack of confidence.

Patti constantly complained about "feeling foolish and stupid," and attributed many of her problems to her lack of education. After a time the group began to lose patience with her and rolled their eyes whenever her self-worth problems became the group's focus. They got tired of hearing her negative self-talk. Finally one of the group members suggested that she really should consider registering for college. "That's ridiculous," Patti said, "I can't afford the tuition and besides, I'm too old to begin." In response the group asked her to consider calling the local college and asking if she could audit one or two classes. In this manner she would not have to pay for the course, she would not have to take tests, but she would also not accumulate any college credits. She said that she was not interested in gathering credits she just wanted to learn and promised the group that she would think about it.

For several weeks, whenever she was asked, Patti said she was still thinking. Then one day Patti came to our session all excited. She told the group that she had enrolled in an Adult Education class to learn how to operate the computer her children had given her for her birthday. She said she will be going one day a week and is looking forward to becoming part of the "computer generation." After a few months had passed the group was aware of a difference in Patti; she had an air of confidence about her and rarely complained about being foolish or stupid. She seemed very proud that she was keeping up with the other students in class and the computer was demystified by her caring and nurturing teacher. As a result, Patti found the Internet to be a wealth of information and knowledge, and her brain was like a sponge, absorbing and processing the material she was so curious about. Patti's group support enabled her and empowered her to find out that you are never too old to learn.

Another support group of women had Adele as a member. She was married for six months when she realized that this man was not for her, so she left and later discovered that she was pregnant. Subsequently she raised her daughter as a single parent for twenty-seven years. A year later her daughter got married and moved to another state to raise her family.

Adele began to attend group a few years ago, following her retirement from the New York City school system, where she worked for 35 years as a secretary in the attendance office of a middle school. In her own words, she said, "I thought I was ready to retire, but I was dead wrong."

What she had envisioned was that she would develop an expansive social life with her neighbors and old friends. The stark reality was that there were no opportunities to develop anything with her neighbors because they were all working or had their own social network. Unmarried now with few hobbies or interests, Adele found herself isolated and lonely. When she found out about the group and made the initial phone call she mentioned that she had recently begun individual therapy. Her therapist suggested that she join a support group to reduce her alienation and see how others handled their loneliness upon retiring. She was anxious to meet other people who had similar life situations that she was experiencing at that time.

Adele seemed like the perfect candidate for a women's group. She was motivated, intelligent and articulate, and had realistic goals for treatment. The other women received her well. They could easily identify with her concerns about retirement, if not from their own personal experience, then from that of their friends, family members and former colleagues. There was more than a sufficient amount of common ground to draw from, and Adele felt the isolation begin to slowly melt away. The group became not only a forum for Adele to share her thoughts and feelings and acquire the support she sorely needed, but also a resource for her to obtain suggestions about what changes to consider in her life. As a result of several months in group and hard, consistent therapeutic work, Adele put some of the suggested ideas into practice. She joined a leisure club, volunteered at a women's shelter one day a week and even tried Internet dating for awhile. The group took on a slightly different purpose once these new behaviors went into motion. Adele now had a safe, warm and encouraging environment in which to talk about her successes, along with her trials and tribulations.

It is very common for the group members to talk about their

adult sons and daughters in Carol's support groups. In one particular group of senior women the subject of relationships with daughters seemed to be the subject that was particularly painful for several of the women. One group member, Emma, had become depressed about the estrangement from her daughter Sonya, who had moved to another county with her husband and two children, reducing the amount of contact they once had from daily to once or twice a month. After many weeks of suggestions about how to help Emma, one of the members of the group asked if she had a webcam. Emma didn't know what that was and they explained that it is a method of utilizing the computer with a little camera device. This camera would enable Emma and her daughter and grandchildren to actually talk to each other and see each other on the computer. If she installed a webcam she would have access to keeping in touch with her family on a more regular basis and might ease her loneliness of not being able to see her grandchildren as they grew. This, of course, did not take the place of a real visit, but it might fill the void between visits for Emma.

Another group member, Sharon, was troubled because her adult daughter furtively blamed her for divorcing her father. Sharon had been in a long-term marriage with a man who was a compulsive gambler. His obsession with gambling was never discussed within the family and his behavior was covered up so well that when Sharon finally sued for divorce it came as a shock to everyone. Still feeling protective of her husband, they had a no-fault divorce and went their separate ways. At this point in her life Sharon joined the group because she needed guidance from the group about how to communicate with her daughter without constantly having the discussion turn into an argument. These arguments often resulted in long periods of silence between them, which was devastating for her. It was suggested by a member of the group that Sharon invite her daughter to a private session with the counselor, to work out their communication problems with a professional in a safe setting. They encouraged her to be honest and open with her daughter in treatment so that they could build a new relationship on a foundation of trust.

A senior woman in another group, Denise, strongly believed that her daughter Emily, who was 55 years old at the time, resented her mother for being totally dependent upon her both financially and emotionally after Emily's father died. The group urged Denise to examine her dependency truthfully and see if her daughter's resentment was based in fact. They encouraged her to look into various methods of financial support that she may be entitled to from social services which would enable her to be more self-sufficient. Since Denise was not physically handicapped in any way, and was an avid reader, they suggested that she volunteer to read to patients in a children's hospital nearby. Over time many of the experiences that other group members shared with her made sense and helped her to explore other options to overcome her excessive dependency on her daughter.

These female group participants were struggling emotionally and the road for each of them did not always lead back to strong family ties initially. However, from the support, encouragement and sharing within the group, if they were willing, each one grew in self-confidence to some extent. The group experience helped them to focus on the part of their life that was simply not working. Although many people fear change, in group they get to the point where their discomfort level is stronger than their fear of change. It is at this point that the dynamics of the group enable them to risk the pain of change for the release of their emotional discomfort. We have seen this dynamic work time and time again, especially in the elderly women in group who have given up hope of being able to change at this late stage of life. The shared experiences of their peers help them to see beyond their limited view and risk moving forward to a more comfortable, rewarding life with their families and friends.

11. Transference and Counter-Transference

The reader can probably imagine that, in working closely in psychotherapy with senior adults, issues of transference and counter-transference are sure to arise and require that the clinician analyze some of them, and, where necessary, seek peer supervision and even their own personal therapy as a forum for addressing it. Katz (1987) claims that the counter-transference for the therapist is a vehicle for growth and individual development and we strongly concur. Katz (1990) suggests that we as clinicians take a step back and a good look at ourselves as we venture on the journey of working with our older patients, as the information we gleam from these analyses take us closer to conceptualizing our patients and identifying the interventions we need to make.

Due to our (the authors') middle age and senior age, it is no surprise that some of the therapy patients came to relate to us as an adult child and in other circumstances, a sibling or as an older parent. Molinari (1996) points out that working with the elderly population can trigger a clinician's own concerns about growing old and Gussaroff (1998) reminds us that clinicians may even avoid delving into the aging patient's deepest feelings as a defense against facing his or her own aging. Let's not also forget that working with older patients arouses a myriad of feelings regarding mortality, death and dying, fears of dependency and separation from adult children and grandchildren, and a host of other feelings as well. For example, Garner (2002) talks about the older person's decreased capability for influencing their environment and Hildebrand (1982) mentions the older individual's feeling that he or she may have failed as a parent.

For therapists working with older patients there are developmental tasks to identify with and also the losses that naturally occur in one's life. As Garner (1982) points out, the "losses occur at any time, but with aging they multiply and accumulate," (p.131). In our practices, we have seen that these multiple losses involve not only people but daily functioning, health, time to spend with loved ones and dreams that go unrealized. The so-called "golden years", as so candidly put by one of our patients, is "often not so golden." Many older individuals feel forced, pressured or resigned to living lifestyles they would not ordinarily choose.

The following is part of an initial interview with an elderly woman who expresses her experience with aging.

> Do you want to know the voice of the elderly? Well let me tell you. It is the voice of tremendous loss. Loss of health, loss of dignity, loss of friends, loss of respect, loss of memory, loss of finances, loss of home and loss of choices, just to name a few! I rely on the calendar on my refrigerator not just to remind me of today's date, but to keep me informed as to which doctor I will be visiting today.
>
> The loss of dignity is something imposed upon me by others. As I age I have lost a few inches in height, so now some people have taken to calling me 'cute'. I find that insulting to a person of my age. To earn the title of 'cute' I believe one must be no older than three or four years, not someone over eighty. Being called 'cute' to me negates any achievements I have earned in my lifetime. I have held very prestigious jobs, earned several college degrees, raised four children, owned property and been celebrated in my profession; so to be called 'cute' is inappropriate and rude.
>
> Many of my friends have moved on; some to Florida, some to Arizona, some to assisted living facilities and some to the great beyond. They are sorely missed and their loss is a constant reminder of my mortality.
>
> Loss of respect strips me of an identity. I become just another number; another grey headed sheep in the flock, like

all the rest. This loss of respect takes the form of being ignored. When my daughter takes me to the doctor, he directs his questions about my health to her, as if I were unseen, unable to speak, think, or answer for myself. I feel myself shrinking and sinking into depression as I feel the sting of age discrimination.

I find it hard to buy something without having to think twice about the cost, or the perceived need; this is another form of loss. Can I do without it? Why do I have to question myself? I am always afraid that my meager savings will be gone and then I fall prey to the deeply dreaded 'Asking my children for help'. I'd rather die…

The home I have lived in for over fifty years is too big for me. I know it and my children know it, but my home brings me comfort. I know where everything is, and I feel secure here. My choices are few: stay where I am, consider assisted living, move in to one of my children's homes, or a small apartment.

Change is very frightening. So often I think to myself: "I've lived long enough." I've seen my children grow up to be responsible adults, with grown children of their own, and I am very proud of them. I know the statement "I've lived long enough" can sound like giving up, but all that looms ahead of me is more and more losses. Why can't I leave now with my health and dignity intact?

My memory is fading. I ask my son, "Did you have a good time at the company party?" He tells me I just asked him five minutes ago. What will happen to me? I fear dementia; I know its devastation first-hand by witnessing both my mother and grandfather losing their memory, losing their mind. Is it happening to me?

Many seniors and elderly adults do not have supportive people in their lives to tell these thoughts and feelings to. Many once did, and now those individuals are gone. Therapy, for some, may be the only environment in which this kind of dialogue takes place. It may also be the rare time the person is listened to and it can therefore become a sacred place for letting these feelings find expression.

With these feelings of loss often come situations such as living with adult children prematurely or when there was no previous plan for the change. In addition to illness or disability, widowhood brings hard to manage changes and adjustments, and often those waters cannot be chartered by the senior or elderly person alone. In addition to that the older patient often has to give up familiar surroundings or material possessions that have great meaning for them, in order to accommodate their needs for safety and security. Moving in with adult children can additionally mean the adjustment of living with a son or daughter-in-law and sometimes their grandchildren, who may be a joy to be with but nonetheless, they present with a faster-paced, sometimes livelier and other times noisier atmosphere than the older parent is comfortable contending with. The senior patients we see can unconsciously stimulate feelings about our own ability to adapt to new surroundings or family situations and they may also tap into current changes we are undergoing and sometimes not finding easy at all to maneuver.

There were many occasions in our practices when our senior patients wanted or needed a family session with one or more adult children. We were especially sensitive to the possibility of that patient having hopes we would take their side and advocate for them with their adult child or children to see their point of view.

Counter-transference, in Garner's terms, may entail the therapist viewing the patient as either a parent, grandparent or a vision of how they see themselves in their older years. The possibilities of what these identifications can arouse are endless. As clinicians, we have witnessed the unfolding of our own counter-transference and have had to obtain peer supervision to work on feelings of sadness, discouragement, anger and pain around issues of aging and mortality. Robiner (n.d.) stresses the importance for therapists working with senior patients to be cognizant of the wide variety of transference projections that can surface during the course of therapy. One of the scenarios highlighted by the author is what he calls "reverse transference". In this dynamic, the older patient attributes characteristics of their adult child to the therapist. This phenomenon often causes the therapist to adopt a negative transference. In fact Robiner describes a full array of emotions and behaviors, such as anger, withdrawal and rebelliousness, that the therapist may engage in, as a result of his or her patient's reverse transference. Another possible scenario suggested by the author is the greater dependency of older patients on therapists. Robiner states that the older patient may "assume a parental or dominant role" with the therapist. The author also warns the clinicians treating older patients against the possibility of treating the patient too delicately due to his or her older years. According to Robiner, the therapist treating the senior patient may shy away from confronting the patient or from taking on a parental role because of the age difference. The reverse side of this, according to Robiner, is the possibility of the patient developing a strong dependency upon the clinician or of reversing the roles in the sense of treating the therapist as though he or she has qualities much like their own adult children.

Gussaroff (1998) also explored the counter-transference held by therapists working with the elderly. The author found that therapists experience feelings about death and dying getting stirred and these feelings may even prevent them from working in depth with their patients. So, some topics get avoided, as in the case of Marla and her daughter Laurie. Marla had just turned 80 and her daughter Laurie was 58 at the time they came in to see me. It was Marla who initiated the discussion of "the will", stating her daughter avoided the subject at all costs. She literally cut her mother off when she raised the issue and cried or left the room when Marla tried to tell her it was important to have her affairs in order at her age. For Marla, it seemed natural to come to a therapist to discuss this. After all, she had been in treatment before, after her husband and she divorced following a long-term marriage. Marla explained that Laurie would not visit an elder law attorney with her and she needed Laurie there to review the financial arrangements, for her funeral and for her will in general, since Laurie was her only child and would be the executor of the will. At the third session, Laurie became much more tolerant of discussing the prospect of going to the lawyer to draw up the needed papers. She was able to express to her mother her fears of losing her and her accompanying fear of becoming the matriarch of the family one day. Marla felt a great deal of compassion, and with the help of a mediator was able to acknowledge her daughter's feelings. The short-term therapy for both of them served to get them past a stuck point, and they were much more comfortable about the legal work that lay ahead.

As a team of authors, with ages that span two decades, we experienced a whole host of feelings in this arena. One of us, being 54, more easily identified with senior patients/parents who are in their seventies and early eighties, while the other being 68, identified with the patients in the mid-eighties. This is not meant to imply that there weren't times in which either one of us didn't relate to a patient of similar years, or even younger, as an adult child, as that certainly also happened. In fact, we acknowledge that in therapy transference and counter-transference knows no age. It has just been more the case that working with patients old enough to be our parents more frequently triggers a counter-transference in which our own parents' qualities are projected. In fact, we agree with Brockett (1991) when the author stresses the importance of introspective-oriented supervision when working with older adults and we were fortunate to have had this highlighted in our supervision so that the analysis of the counter-transference, and all the knowledge it affords us, is not minimized or neglected in our work.

One of our patients, a woman in her early seventies, was complaining about how she noticed a marked progression of "forgetfulness", accompanied by feelings of anger, frustration and shame. Her strongest feeling when she became forgetful was fear. She had been witness to her grandfather's dementia when she was a child, and her mother's Alzheimer's twenty years ago. She vividly recalled how her mother begged her to help her end her life if she "became demented like father." Now that the patient was experiencing similar symptoms, she was paralyzed with thoughts that she had the same disease. In listening to the patient share her fear, a chord struck in the therapist's mind about her own fears of becoming victim of Alzheimer's disease. Feeling increasingly uncomfortable each time this patient spoke about her forgetfulness, the therapist scheduled an appointment for peer supervision.

Another one of our patients, a woman in her eighties, agreed to a joint session with her 62-year-old daughter, as they were going through a tough time deciding whether they could agree to live together, now that they were both widowed. The whole concept of living together as older adults struck yet another chord with Barbara, who had been living with her own mother at the time. Carol and Barbara are fortunate to have each other at these kinds of clinical junctures. That way, any counter-transference related material that arises can be explored with professional confidentiality in place. This case represents one of those examples where peer supervision can assist while performing a kind of check and balance of a therapist's feelings. For example, Barbara wanted to make sure she didn't feel she in any way imposed her values about living with and caring for an elderly parent onto Dana and her daughter. After talking to Carol, and exploring various options with mother and daughter, Barbara realized that Dana and her daughter were looking for a temporary solution in terms of a shared residence, not a long-term arrangement. The emotional load was lightened for both of them once they defined the limits of the change they were seeking.

This above scenario is not uncommon when working with older adults and their aging relatives. Therapists often identify with emotions that their patient shares in treatment. Some of the feelings they experience are painful and create conflict, particularly when they involve fears and anticipatory anxiety about aging and the finality of life. We have found that peer supervision can be extremely useful in such cases and we have therefore called upon each other to review our work and the feelings that surface with individual patients.

12. Older and Wiser

Many of our patients are in their older years and therefore there are a large percentage of people in long-term marriages within our practices. Of course, we recognize that we are living in the 2000's and therefore we also see many second and even third marriages in the patients we treat. For those cases in which the couple has had only one marriage lasting more than 35 years, we have come to learn some very special features about sustaining a marital connection through change, adjustment, loss and growth.

Sharlin & Kaslow (2000) claim that older couples that stay together for 20-40 years, through "thick and thin (as the name of their book suggests)", do so in part because they interpret crises as challenges or opportunities for growth. Those couples in long-term marriages, interviewed by the authors, also thrived in their relationships due to their ability to problem solve and become resourceful as a couple team. In a review of the research literature addressing characteristics of long-term marriages, Sharlin & Kaslow (2000) mention an international study conducted in the early 90's. One of the authors (Kaslow) participated in that study and found that all of the twenty couples interviewed felt their common interest in their children was essential in their lives. Those couples who felt dissatisfied with their marriages identified having children as one of the reasons to explain the longevity of their marriage.

According to Henry, Berg, Smith & Florsheim (2007), older marriages are characterized by more positive behaviors (i.e. increasingly more affection and better communication) than seen in middle age marriages. Carstensen, Gottman, & Levenson (1995) agree that older couples in long-term marriages are more affectionate than middle-aged couples and they also express less negativity, even when ironing out their differences. Our practice experience has confirmed this notion.

Many of our older patients have shared stories of positive change in their marriages and these shifts occurred after the couples surpassed the first thirty or forty years together. When exploring the permanence of these relationships, we consistently heard our older patients stress the importance of communication certainly, but that was not the only contributor to their happiness. These couples also seem to believe that priorities change when people spend many years together married. The ones that they mentioned most are the needs for companionship, quick conflict resolution and family stability. As one of our patients said during a marital session, "It is a sheer waste of time to argue about the little things, and even the big things, as time is precious to us now." Another male in a long-term live-in relationship offered the following advice to other older couples: "History cannot ever be replaced by a new attraction, and real commitment is the best aphrodisiac." He was definitely giving the world the message that people should make every effort to stay together if there is substantive relating between them, during a course of many years, as new relationships don't offer the same familiarity, connection and experience.

Many of the older couples we treat have shared with us the positive effect their relationships have had upon their children and eventually upon their grandchildren as well. One senior father told us that he liked to think of his marriage as a "good, healthy couple role model" for his two daughters, ages 42 and 45, who each married and seemed well on their way to marriages with longevity too. Susan, a senior lady one of us worked with, put it this way: "There is a definite correlation between my 40-year marriage and my children's values about marriage for themselves." Susan added that it was the communication with her husband that also extended to her adult children that paved the way for compatible, satisfying marriages with their partners.

Long-terms marriages often imply deeper connections to family members as well. Hargrave & Anderson (1992) talk about the "intense loyalty" found in intergenerational families. These authors attempt to dispel the myth about the extended family having deteriorated. In fact the research team contends that aging parents and their adult children are more involved with each others' lives today than they were generations ago. They add that aging parents also live with (or near) their adult children in many more circumstances than most would believe.

In our clinical practices, we have seen many families who are close and others who are overly dependent upon one another. In the former, they share a very strong, healthy bond and it spans across a few generations of family members. These family units seem to function very fluidly, with grandparents helping parents with childcare and middle-aged sons and daughters caring for their elderly parents as well. Sometimes the families live together, and at other times close by.

It is an amazing phenomenon that in this era of rampant divorces and disposable marriages that there should be a significant proportion of long-term marriages as well. I had the distinct pleasure of interviewing such a couple, married an unbelievable 75 years.

Bertha and Herman Solomon were married June 3, 1933 in Brooklyn, and for the past three years have resided in the Atria at Great Neck, New York (a Senior Living community). At the tender age of 17 Herman worked for Bertha's brother Leo. Leo asked Herman if he would take his kid sister to the movies. The rest is history! They dated for a few years before they married and settled in Williamsburg for a few years, and then moved to their home in Forest Hills where they resided for 54 years.

They described their relationship with their two daughters, Sharon and Sheila. When they were young children, Herman said that he was the breadwinner and Bertha was the disciplinarian. "I taught my daughters what they would have to face in the future, and how to be self-sufficient and independent," said Bertha. She provided her girls with solid boundaries and raised them with the humanistic values of respect and familial cooperation. This formed a strong bond between the four.

When Herman was diagnosed with ulcers in 1952, Bertha poured over medical books until she developed a healthy diet, not only for Herman's condition, but one that the whole family would be able to benefit from. As a result, they have all formed and acquired healthy eating habits that they still adhere to.

Later on, when their daughters married and moved away, one to upstate New York and the other to Arizona, the closeness that they had developed in the early years continued to thrive. Judith Richlin-Klonsky and Vern L. Bengston, in their article, "Pulling Together, Drifting Apart: A Longitudinal Case Study of a Four-Generation Family", published in the Journal of Aging Studies, 08904065, Vol. 10, Issue 4, cite varying information in their Geographic and Interpersonal Distance segment on the Potter family. "Although a few Potter family members use geographic distance as a barrier to family interactions, their closeness or disaffection cannot be predicted by geography alone." This finding raises important issues regarding the recurring debate in the gerontological research literature regarding the effect of geographical distance on contact between adult children and their elderly parents (DeWitt and Frankel 1988, p.26). The Potters represent a case in which increased distance does not necessarily result in decreased support: a few other family members who live far away are given extensive assistance. But the family also demonstrates that proximity in itself does not necessarily lead to or predict increased contact, since some family members are routinely ignored."

We find that some family members move away from their elderly parents to increase their geographic distance because they want to detach themselves from family members. It seems like the old saying, 'Which came first, the chicken or the egg?' also can apply to people who purposely relocate far away from family because of a desire for decreased contact, instead of the implication that their decreased contact was being determined by distance. In the history of the Solomon family, the exact opposite holds true. Another example of their daughters' sense of devotion to their parents, even though they geographically separated, is the following:

While at their vacation condo in Palm Springs, California, Bertha fell and broke her arm. Her two daughters immediately flew down to be with them and brought them to New York for the surgery. While she was hospitalized, the girls went back to their parents' condo, packed up their things, gave the condo to a realtor, and told their parents that they thought it would not be wise for them to be alone anymore. At this point, Herman and Bertha welcomed this decision, and the girls eventually sold their home in Forest Hills as well as their condo in California. While their mother was rehabilitating, the sisters visited many, many assisted living communities. When they brought their parents to visit their number one choice, they all finally decided upon the Atria in Great Neck. Bertha and Herman have been there happily for several years.

Sharlin, Kaslow and Hammerschmidt, in their book "Together through Thick and Thin," (Haworth Clinical Practice Press, 2000), state that an essential ingredient in successful marriages is the element of fun. Many of the couples they interviewed for their book reported a strong, lifelong friendship described as spending enjoyable time together engaged in mutually satisfying activities. They said that their appreciation of the sense of closeness and comfort they felt with each other has grown stronger over time. These couples still find each other attractive and they value the sexual aspect of their relationship.

Herman and Bertha are still active and alert at 98 years and 97 years respectively, and they are an inspiration to others in the community. They have two daughters, four grandchildren and seven great-grandchildren that they adore and who visit them frequently. When asked to describe any conflicts in their marriage over time, Bertha remarked, "My husband loves all kinds of sports on TV. He watches baseball, football, basketball, you name it, and he enjoys it. In the earlier years of our marriage I would resent him watching all these ball games." Herman interjected by saying, "Yes, but now you watch the ball games with me and you enjoy them too!" At which Bertha rolled her eyes and said, "I watch them with you, but I don't enjoy them!"

At the 75th Anniversary Party at the Atria, both Sharon and Sheila spoke about the fact that all their lives their parents have been there for them and it is comforting to know when they wake up each day that they are still there for them. These two daughters did not refer to any role reversal that many other adult children raise; as a shift in many other children's relationships with their aging parents often creates a shift of power and responsibility from parent to child. Instead, Sharon and Sheila, with a definite tone of humility and appreciation, referred to their family of origin as one that has maintained the very distinct roles of parent and child, even into the latter years of life. It sounds like an extremely healthy model to us and reminds us of a statement made by Morris (1996) when discussing the aging family and role status of aging parents and their adult children: "Not only should you avoid parenting your parent, but go a step further: make a point of strengthening his independence...... Your role now is not to control your parent's life, but to help him maintain control of it."

The first phone contact with Ronnie and Bill Carlucci was a great sneak preview of a journey down memory lane with a very special couple and their family. The Carlucci's are unique in that they have been married for 74 years and can say "happily" when they refer to their union. In fact, their youngest daughter Lynne heartily agrees and even adds that her parents got along well all throughout her childhood.

We first contacted Bill and Ronnie at their adult residence in September of 2007. It was an interesting experience just getting in touch. The director of Cedar Creek adult residential facility in Crystal River, Florida, was initially reached by phone and then called the Carlucci's room to ask if they would like to receive a call from Dr. Barbara Kaplan, one of the authors of a book on aging parents and their adult children, who wanted to interview them. After Bill and Ronnie agreed to accept the call, Dr. Kaplan was notified and then spoke with each of them briefly. It was explained that, due to the fact that they are married this length of time and have very positive experiences to share about parent and child relationships, a chapter would be dedicated to them, to symbolize what a family can strive for and to inspire those who have become discouraged about their family lacking closeness and cohesion.

The stories we have to share, that are derived from our clinical work, discuss a myriad of problems adult children and their senior parents have relating at this stage in the life cycle. The individuals we see come to us for help in resolving these problems and we feel blessed to say that we have had good results, yet a story from a couple in their nineties, who each cannot even recall a family problem too insurmountable to solve, is a true story of hope and promise that we chose to use as the most suitable end to our book.

We never would have met the Carlucci's if it weren't for Pamela Joy. I met Pamela one day during the summer of 2006 and she told me she was moved by her friend Lynne's parents', a couple whose marriage was still going strong after 74 years. Pamela added that Bill and Ronnie Carlucci have wonderful parent-child relationships with their two daughters Elaine (age 74) and Lynne (age 54). In fact, their favorite times of all are spent during the visits from their adult daughters and their families, which happen quite frequently. I contacted Lynne, their daughter, by phone and we both felt comfortable with one another from the outset. She was eager to have Carol and I read an article written about her parents in a local Florida paper. The article presented the loving, tender relationship Bill and Ronnie Carlucci still possess and it described the typical scene at the center: The Carlucci's interact with their friends each morning and later in the day, Bill listens to Ronnie play piano and the two of them sit outside on the porch holding hands at the culmination of the evening.

The Carlucci's agreed to be interviewed but the interview needed to be assisted by Lynne, their youngest daughter, as sometimes either Bill or Ronnie feel a bit challenged in terms of their memories. Lynne is able to help her parents remember details of their past by providing key words or triggers to aid them along. Carol and I went to Lynne's home, in Long Island, a suburb of New York, in November and we sat around her dinner table with her husband Bob and began our interview with their fond reminiscences of their memories of Lynne's childhood experiences growing up and their courtship and subsequent marriage. Then we called Ronnie and Bill as a time was set aside for conducting a three-way phone conversation.

Bill and Ronnie sounded proud to tell us that they are married 74 years and have no regrets. They explained their belief that their relationships with their two adult daughters are without problems because they had them 20 years apart. We chuckled, only because it is such a big age difference and it was especially delightful to hear Bill add "we certainly had to get it right after twenty years!"

The authors alternately spoke with each of the Carlucci's. Bill told us that he and Ronnie presently have no major health problems, a true blessing for them at their ages. Their marriage is strong, which they both agree is a function of a lasting love, and their only significant romantic love experience. Neither recalled any period of time in which they were not talking to one another or stopped communicating with either of their daughters. The first word uttered by Bill when we mentioned Elaine's name and asked about their relationship was "swell", and an inquiry as to what he felt about Lynne resulted in the key word "angel".

There has in recent years been many times in which both Elaine and Lynne felt they would like Bill and Ronnie to live with one of them. In fact, prior to moving into the senior residence, Lynne and her husband Bob asked the Carlucci's if they would consider a move up North but they declined and Lynne feels it was due to the weather differences between Florida and New York. Once they moved into the facility and developed friendships with other residents, and, according to Lynne, "tasted the food," they were hooked on Crystal Creek! Both Lynne and Bob agreed that additionally, Lynne's parents do like their independence. The notion of having them move in with Lynne and Bob at a later point, if needed, remains an "open door policy."

According to Ronnie, she and Bill felt fortunate that finances were manageable and also attributed it to being a two-income family. The only debated item in anything reported by the Carlucci's was Lynne's insistence that she was "a handful" as a teenager but her parents minimized that, almost as though no parenting stage presented hardship for either of them. When we asked the Carlucci's how they explain the ease with which their family got along and the endurance of their marital relationship all these years, Ronnie said that, "The blessings come from the Lord," and that faith and love was all they needed.

In their book, "Together through Thick and Thin", authors Sharlin, Kaslow and Hammerschmidt report that healthy families and satisfying long-term marriages are also characterized by shared values, either brought to the marriage by one of the partners or evolving together over the years. A belief in something bigger than self or family that is worth committing oneself to was noted by many. This type of belief system, often said to be a spiritual dimension, was thought to be a very important aspect of the solidarity and success of their marriages.

We spoke to Lynne some more after completing the interview

with her parents and she confirmed that her parents' strong religious faith was an enduring element in her family system. She revealed that her parents had a third child, a son, two years before she was born, who died at childbirth. This tragedy, which might have shaken a less spiritual couple, only strengthened their union and they continued valiantly to forge ahead in their relationship.

One might think that this story of the memories of a couple married 74 years is too good to be true. If you consider that there is a chance that they only remember all the good times of their marriage and the other memories may have been cast aside to the far recesses of their minds, isn't that in itself a blessing of old age? Who are we to judge?

Conclusion

When we began to write this book many of our colleagues voiced concern that working with the elderly would be discouraging, frustrating and unrewarding. They declared that this population is "too stubborn and set in their ways." They further stated that in working with them it would be impossible to attain any morsel of satisfaction in our work. To our delight we were able to prove how truly wrong they were. As a result, one of our goals for writing this book became our desire to dispel the myth that it's depressing and disheartening to work with the elderly. Instead we found the work uplifting and inspiring and learned there is hope, wisdom, knowledge, strength, honesty and resiliency with this population.

Our second goal in writing this book is for our patients to define how they want their life's ending to be, and what they are willing to do to achieve their objective. It is our honor to be their guides on this journey.

Our third goal is for clinicians, people who do mental health counseling, to shed new light on a topic that has had little or no emphasis in the field. We also want to share our own clinical approaches that have been successful with this age group.

In our work on the book we found that growth and change are on a continuum and do not end until you draw your last breath. The people we worked with were honest, open and willing to share their stories and accept constructive criticism to improve areas where they may have fallen short of their conception of the 'ideal parent'. They were able to be flexible and embrace new ideas in order to change for the positive.

We found that sometimes therapeutic progress appears in small ways and requires even smaller steps, such as helping an elderly person function well on a daily basis. At other times, therapy unravels complex dynamics in the patient's family relationships that need attention, sorting out and an eventual change. Usually they uncover a change that is welcomed, if not initiated, by the patient.

Many of our patients were at a stage in life where they 'looked back' over their lives and were unhappy with some of the decisions they had made in the past. Men especially had regrets and were feeling guilty that they may have put their careers before their families. In countless cases, during and after therapy sessions, the aging parents wanted to make amends to their children for their behavior in the past, and were able to reconcile the past and reunite with them. The senior/elderly patients also wanted to express, with a newly acquired *voice*, thoughts and feelings that had been either squelched or went unnoticed for many years. In this way, new dialogues were able to be opened and we, as clinicians, were pleased to facilitate new ways for parents and adult children to communicate and feel understood.

Often the elderly parent takes stock of the things in their life that went well and those things that they regret, or may feel guilt or remorse for the relationships within the family that they failed to nurture and develop. The words to the song, "Cat's in the Cradle", come back to haunt the men of the 50's, 60's and 70's who tried to build a career, very often at the expense of bonding and forming a relationship with their young children. Now that they are retired and have the time to review their lives, they mourn the loss of a meaningful connection with their children that they feel they sacrificed for the sake of their careers. They sadly say, "I did it for them," but the reality is that their children suffered in the process and now they are all suffering the loss.

As authors, both of us learned a great deal about the aging process in recording these experiences in this book. It has been a refreshing and exhilarating process for us to document the often unheard voice of the aging parent in their relationships with their family and add to the literature that had previously lacked the many insights we witnessed. It has been our pleasure observing our patients willingness to change in order to facilitate a more rewarding, worthwhile and satisfying relationship with their children in their later years. We're happy to report that, on countless occasions, we encountered a reversal of the old adage, 'You can't teach old dog new tricks.'

We discovered that given the opportunity to view their negative, critical, destructive communication and interaction with their family and children as being harmful and detrimental to their quality of life as they aged, they were willing and able to learn and embrace affirmative, clear-cut, explicit techniques that would enrich these relationships and help to close the chasm which may have existed for years between them and their offspring. In essence they became our 'role models' for aging.

Listening to our patients express strong feelings about the aging process is a great privilege and a great responsibility. To deal with these types of intense feelings one cannot issue platitudes such as, "There, there, things will get better dear. Just hang in there." We believe that our role in counseling mature people is to deal in the reality of life, and help our patients see that there is joy to be found in aging. In many of the experiences we've heard from the aging population, it may be just that the losses are more easily seen and identified and the joys may be harder to define. That is what makes our job so challenging. Being able to listen empathetically and compassionately to the pain and suffering in our patients' lives and then become guides to enable and empower our patients to identify the activities and relationships that bring them happiness is an honor that we cherish. In a selfish way, we understand that their voices may very well be our voices in the future, so we are both teachers and students of life at the very same time. Discovering that they are literally never too old to learn new and improved communication skills and become willing to abandon the negative style that didn't work for them any longer is what continued to spark our excitement and interest.

The challenge that we sometimes faced was to present their off-putting behaviors to our patients in a non-judgmental, constructive framework in order to motivate them to change. It was their challenge to accept our methods of change as a means of creating a positive, healthy environment for them to live out the rest of their lives, surrounded by their family in harmony. As one of our patients said, "I don't need a fortune, a fancy car or a palace to be happy. All I need is to live in peace with myself knowing I did the best I could, and feeling secure in the fact that I love others fully and that the significant others in my life love me."

Getting the message that adult children need a different kind of parenting is not an easy thing to digest, therefore we rejoice in knowing that our senior patients use therapy as a way of gaining new tools of communication for successful parenting and interacting with siblings and friends. We have seen our patients exhibit a tremendous amount of courage and determination to evolve into softer, more accepting people. It is tremendously hard to change, especially when you reach 'a certain age', but it is never too late to examine what doesn't work in your life and make the necessary adjustments and tweak that which needs to be tweaked. When our patients felt that their quality of life was not fulfilling or satisfying, they were not adverse to looking within themselves, without pointing blame onto others, and correcting the situation. That is why we refer to many of our patients as "role models"!

Our book is not about how adult children interact with their parents as much as how their elderly parents relate to them at this late stage of their lives. As we stated before, most of our patients view this stage of their lives as the *final curtain* in a play. Will they experience joy and have their ending be one that will be productive and beneficial in their relationships with their children, or will it filled with pain and be destructive and overflowing with bitterness? With therapy they learn that the choice is really theirs.

As for our *choice,* we will continue to work with this population, one which we very much enjoy. We expect to find more direction from our clinical experience and from our patients' stories to share with the mental health professional community so that the aging parent's voice will finally and clearly be heard.

Bibliography

Bly, S.A. (1993). Once a Parent Always a Parent: How to Love and Support Your Adult Children. Illinois: Tyndale House Publishers.

Brabant, S. (1996). Mending the Torn Fabric: For Those Who Grieve and Those Who Want to Help Them. Amityville, New York: Baywood Publishing Company, Inc.

Brockett, D.R. (1991). Countertransference with the Older Adult: The Importance of Mental Health Counselor Awareness and Strategies for Effective Management. Journal of Mental Health Counseling, 13(3), 343-355.

Carstensen, L., Gottman, J. & Levenson, R.(1995) Emotional Behavior in Long-term Marriage. Psychology and Aging, 10(1).

Clarke, E., Preston, M., Raksin, J. & Bengston, V. (1999). Types of Conflict and Tensions Between Older Parents and Adult Children. The Gerontologist, 39(3), 261-270.

Coleman, J. (2007). When Parents Hurt: Compassionate Strategies When You and Your Grown Child Don't Get Along. New York: Harper Collins Publishers.

Crowther, M.R. & Zeiss, A.M. (2006, August). Cognitive-behavior Therapy in Older Adults: A Case Involving Sexual Functioning. Journal of Clinical Psychology, 55(8), 961-975.

Donofrio, L.M. & Sheehan, N.W. (2001). Relationship Dynamics Between Aging Mothers and Caregiving Daughters: Filial Expectations and Responsibilities. Journal of Adult Development, 8(1), 39-49.

Finley, N.J., Roberts, D. & Banahan, B. (1988). Motivators and Inhibitors of Attitudes Filial Obligation Toward Aging Parents. The Gerontologist, 28(1), 73-78.

Frankel, D. & Dewit, B (1989, Summer). Geographic Distance and Intergenerational Contact: An Empirical Examination of the

Relationship. Journal of Aging Studies, 3(2), 139-162.

Garner, J. (2002). Psychodynamic Work and Older Adults. Advances in Psychiatric Treatment, 8, 128-135.

Gershenfeld, M.K. (1992, November). Adult Children and Their Parents: The Ties that Keep on Binding. USA Today Magazine, 121(2570), 66-69.

Golish, T. (2000, Summer). Changes in Closeness Between Adult Children and Their Parents: A Turning Point Analysis. Communication Reports, 13(2), 79-98.

Gussaroff, E. (1998). Denial of Death and Sexuality in the Treatment of Elderly Patients. Psychoanalysis and Psychotherapy, 15(1), 77-91.

Hargrave, T.D. & Anderson, W.T. (1992). Finishing Well: Aging and Reparation in the Intergenerational Family. New York: Brunner Mazel, Inc.

Henry, N., Berg, C., Smith, T.& Florsheim, P. (2007). Positive and Negative Characteristics of Marital Interaction and Their Association with Marital Satisfaction in Middle-aged and Older Couples. Psychology and Aging, 22(3), 428-441.

Herzog, J.M. 2001). Father Hunger: Explorations with Adults and Children. Hillsdale, N.J.: The Analytic Press.

Horney, K. (1993). Our Inner Conflicts: A Constructive Theory of Neurosis. New York: W.W. Norton & Company.

Ikkink, K., Van Tilburg, T. & Knipscheer, K. (1999, November). Perceived Instrumental Support Exchanges in Relationships Between Elderly Parents and Their Adult Children: Normative and Structural Expectations. Journal of Marriage and Family, 61(4).

Ingersoll-Dayton, B. (2001, July). Aging Parents Helping Adult Children: The Experience of the Sandwiched Generation. Family Relations, 50(3), 262-271.

Isay, J. (2007).Walking on Eggshells. New York: Doubleday Flying Dolphin Press

Johnson, A.L. (2005).Adult Children of Aging Parents: A Guide for Counselors. American Counseling Association [ACA], 93-97

Johnson, A.L. (2005). Article 19: Adult Children of Aging Parents: A Guide for Counselors. American Counseling Association: Retrieved from the Internet: Vistas Online, September 2, 2007, 93-97).

Katz, R.S. (1987, Spring). Older People, Dying and Countertransference. Generations: Journal of the American Society on Aging, 11(3). Special Issue: Death and Bereavement, 28-32.

Katz, R.S. (1990). Using Our Emotional Reactions to Older Patients: A Working Theory. In Countertransference and Older patients. Thousand Oaks, CA: Sage Publications, p.17-26.

Knight, B.G. (1996).Psychotherapy with Older Adults (2nd ed.). Thousand Oaks, California; Sage Publications.

Kraus, C.A., Kunik, M.E. & Stanley, M.A. (2007, June). Use of Cognitive Behavioral Therapy in Late-life Psychiatric Disorders. Geriatrics, 62(6), 21-26.

Luescher, K., & Pillemer, K. (1998, May). Intergenerational Ambivalence: A New Approach to the Study of Parent-child Relations in Later Life. Journal of Marriage and the Family, 60(2).

Mancini, J.A., Blieszner, R. (1989, May). Aging Parents and Adult Children: Research Themes in Intergenerational Relations. Journal of Marriage and the Family, 51: 275- 290.

Molinari, V. (1996). Current Approaches to Therapy with Elderly Patients. The Hatherleigh Guide to Psychotherapy: pp.193-213. New York: Hatherleigh Press.

Montoro, J. (1994).Cooperation and Competition Among Aged Parents and Adult Children. Ann Arbor, Michigan: Dissertation published.

Morris, V. (1996). How to Care for Aging Parents. New York: Workman Publishing.

Nemzoff, R. (2008). Don't Bite Your Tongue. New York: Palgrave Macmillan.

Park, K., Phua, V. & McNally, J. (2005). Diversity and Structure of Intergenerational Relationships: Elderly Parent–Adult Child Relations in Korea. Journal of Cross-Cultural Gerontology, 20, 285-305.

Pyke, K. (1999, August). The Micropolitics of Care in Relationships Between Aging Parents and Adult Children: Individualism, Collectivism, and Power. Journal of Marriage and the Family, 661-672.

Richlin-Klonsky, J., Bengston, V. (1996, Winter.) Pulling Together, Drifting Apart: A Longitudinal Case Study of a Four-generation Family. Journal of Aging Studies, 10(4),255-279.

Robiner, W.N. (n.d.) An Experimental Inquiry into Roles and Age. Retrieved online 9/30/07.

Satre, D.D., Knight, B.G., David, S. (2006, October). Cognitive-behavioral Interventions with Older Adults: Integrating Clinical and Gerontological Research. Professional Psychology: Research and Practice, 37(5), 489-498.

Secunda, V. (2000). Losing Your Parents, Finding Yourself. New York: Hyperion.

Shapiro, A. (2004). Revisiting the Generation Gap: Exploring the Relationships of Parent/Adult-Child Dyads. International Journal of Aging and Human Development, 58(2), 127-146.

Sharlin, S.A., Kaslow, F.W., Hammerschmidt, H. (2000). Together Through Thick and Thin: A Multinational Picture of Long-term Marriages. New York: Haworth Clinical Practice Press.

Sherrell, K., Buckwalter, K.C. & Morhardt, D. (2001, August). Negotiating Family Relationships: Dementia Care as a Midlife Developmental Task. Families in Society, 82(4), 383-392.

Silverstein, M. & Bengston, V.L. (1994). Does Intergenerational Social Support Influence the Psychological Well-being of Older Parents? The Contingencies of Declining Health and Widowhood. Social Science Medicine, 38(7), 943-957.

Spillers, C.S. (2007, August). An Existential Framework for Understanding the Counseling Needs of Patients. American Journal of Speech-Language Pathology. 16, 191-197.

Turcotte, M.(2006, Spring). Parents with Adult Children Living at Home. Canadian Social Trends, Catalogue No.11-008.

Umberson, D. (1992, August). Relationships Between Adult Children and Their Parents: Psychological Consequences for Both Generations. Journal of Marriage and Family, 54(3).

Van Gaalen, R. & Dykstra, P. (2006, November). Solidarity and Conflict Between Adult Children and Parents: A Latent Analysis. Journal of Marriage and Family, 947-960.

Willson, A.E., Shuey, K.M., Elder, G.H., Jr. (2003, November). Ambivalence in the Relationship of Adult Children to Aging Parents and In-laws. Journal of Marriage and Family, 65(4), 1055-1072.

Yalom, I. (1989). Love's Executioner and Other Tales of Psychotherapy. New York: Basic Books.